GETTING THROUGH CUSTOMS

FROM ONE STATE TO ANOTHER

SOPHIA TELLEN

GETTING THROUGH CUSTOMS

Copyright © Sophia Tellen, 2011

© Updated edition 2016

ISBN 978-0-557-11093-3

Published by Tellen Books, Switzerland

FOR YOU,

WHO ALSO HAVE A STORY TO TELL

GETTING THROUGH CUSTOMS

CONTENTS

GETTING THROUGH CUSTOMS

ACKNOWLEDGEMENTS

I have very much appreciated the support of two remarkable and most generous friends: Pamela Vidal and Emmanuel Power, in particular for their patient reading of ongoing versions over a prolonged period of time and for their helpful comments.

I am indebted to the Geneva Writers' Group and in particular Susan Tiberghien, Founder and Director, Wallis Wilde-Menozzi and D-L. Nelson for advice and encouragement.

I am grateful to Larry Habegger, Travelers' Tales Executive Editor, for his editorial support and advice.

My gratitude also goes to Jim Cooper, whose literary and cultural awareness, and astute advice was a generous gift.

Thank you Ania Mudrewicz for permission to use your Seychelles photographs. Joyful thanks, too, to my niece, Monique A. Sannes, whose superb skills came to my rescue more than once.

Likewise much gratitude goes to Anni Schönbörner-Mauve, my faithful proof-reader.

GETTING THROUGH CUSTOMS

INTRODUCTION

Getting Through Customs is a travel memoir consisting of fifteen true stories centered on transition, and evoking many border crossings: cultural and psychological, as well as geographical. I have woven together my *early*, *middle* and *late* experience. The three sections correspond roughly to different periods of my life: the *early* up to the age of twenty, the *middle* till fifty, and the *late crossings* thereafter. But time circles: the same story may also embed memories of an earlier period. Each story steps through the door of the present to peer into a moment of the past; some of such "moments" can span fifty years.

The Second World War uprooted a generation of Europeans, and numerous border crossings followed. The geographical crossings in this book illustrate how some of us adapted. Other crossings are cultural or mental transitions and evolving emotional states. All these moves are both important and touch the essential.

However, this collection does not purport to

be an autobiography, but it sets out to highlight certain moments of experience, to provide glimpses into the travels that "travelled me" – places in which life placed me - as well as those I consciously chose to visit - to create a pause, retune and regenerate. Some places were points of peace; others held uncanny power.

Implicit within each story is the lesson learned, the gift received. From Cairo to Cape Town, Geneva to Singapore, from Boston to Barbados, the lessons in these transitions were numerous: the need to drop expectations and to step out of the territory of illusion; that setting out too soon exacts a price; that one cannot believe all one is told, even by *Authority,* and that one always remains free to look for the blessing in compelling experience. I learned to look without judging, to smile at my youthful naiveté, and to accept what life has to offer.

Likewise, the gifts of travel were many: finding inspiration in otherness and similarities in the differences; discovering hearts open and ready to care; seeing the miracle in the ordinary, slipping out of time into the Mystery where time is not; and learning to look with the eyes of wonder.

But it was sheer passion that led me to discover the Greek islands and the Seychelles.

Particular magic lay in reconnecting with friendships forged long ago and finding they had outlasted time; in setting out as a stranger and discovering a new sense of family; in moving from the state of being a perpetual foreigner, towards feeling at home wherever life has placed me.

It is my hope that this book will encourage readers to tell their own stories, to rekindle their capacity for youthful wonder, to dare to dare, to share, to laugh, to cry, to remember, to tap the sap of their own wisdom and to ignite the enthusiasm that fans the fire of their own creativity.

In this process I invite you, dear reader, to join me.

Sophia Tellen
Geneva
Switzerland
January 2016

Getting Through Customs

PROLOGUE

Stories are queuing up, shouting, clamoring, quarrelling; some patient, some not.

Some are English. These queue silently, patiently, mutely, under their life yoke, without complaint.

Some queue French-style - like the drivers stopped at crossroads by a policeman desperately blowing out his lungs in sharp shrills of whistle, holding up the cars from all directions - drivers who get out and shout back at him, and at one another. These don't have time to wait.

And some, like me, act like a foreigner in Israel, who waits patiently at the bus stop in the sun, one hour before the bus is due. Then suddenly, as the air fills with diesel, multi-people surge in from nowhere - shoving, pushing, crowding out the solitary queuer - and filling the bus full.

This solitary queuer finds herself suddenly last as the bus begins to roar. Some kind fellow takes in the scene and shouts,

"Stick your elbows out and shove hard, if you want to get on!"

The law-abiding queuer jabs her elbows into the jostling pushers at that Israeli bus stop. That story, too, will get written - though last - with the hem of its skirt caught in the snap of automatic doors.

Stories are queuing, shouting, clamoring, quarrelling;

some patient, some not.

falling over their own feet, half-sleepy,

awakened by a sudden something they cannot name,

they cannot resist.

They cannot all get themselves written, all at once.

So they complain:

We are waiting! We are waiting!

Fetch us, now that we're awake!

As they crowd around my shoulders some whisper, some clamor, some merely suggest,

Name Us!

Claim Us!

We're ready to be freed!

Stories tumble out of years, and months, and moments: out of muscles, skin and viscera; they burst out of their cells, white or red, or altogether nondescript. So long inscribed, they are ready now to follow the call that will lead them out of their body-mind world.

Suddenly I discover, wide-eyed, that I am inhabited by these denizens who shout at me,

"At least put down our *names*!"

EARLY CROSSINGS

GETTING THROUGH CUSTOMS

Mr. Kyriakos has No Vegetables

It was in South Africa, in Cape Town, that we discovered we belonged to different species: Foreigners. *Uitlanders,* in Afrikaans.

To begin with, no one could say our name; no one even got near it. The milkman passed daily on his rounds, leaving the bottles of milk, cream and eggs on our doorstep. With them we would find, scrawled on a scrap of paper, some variation of our name that vaguely suggested it might be us. We had never had this problem before and began to feel like some curiosity, even to ourselves. Every week there was a new surprise as we opened the front door.

Vegetables - rarely fresh enough to please my mother - were delivered by Mr. Kyriakos, the Greek, usually in a tatty cardboard box. He, too, would leave them on our doorstep with a special edition of our name. Greengrocers were often Greeks, and Greeks also had *names*, so we didn't mind as much when a curious new version of our name came from him. Mr. Kyriakos delivered the vegetables himself, and my mother found this very convenient.

But every time, and without fail, my mother

would lament: "Kyriakos has no vegetables."

Mr. Kyriakos was always shuffling around in thick leather sandals and shunting heavy crates this way and that with his strong, grimy hands. As he bent down, the wiry hairs on his back curled out of his T-shirt. His heavy, square gold wristwatch offset his olive skin. As far as I was concerned, Mr. Kyriakos had all the vegetables one could possibly dream of. But inevitably my mother lamented, "Kyriakos has no vegetables."

My father was a vegetarian and believed in *Rohkost* – 80% of his daily diet was made up of raw salads - and he drank fresh carrot juice every day. Before she got a juicer, my mother used to grate the carrots and squeeze the juice out of them by hand. But as a child, I found my mother's complaint incomprehensible.

My mother had often sent me out by bicycle to scout where else fresh vegetables might be available that week. And I was always puzzled as to why she was never happy with what I found. The Greek and Portuguese greengrocers were not far away. Their stores held an amazing array of vegetables, shelf upon shelf, with more crates at the back. Colors quibbled with each other for importance; eggplants clamored for attention next to the sweet-smelling lemons and pineapples. The Portuguese whistled more than the Greek; but my mother thought just as poorly of his vegetables! But nevertheless, it was always to the Greek Mr. Kyriakos that she sent me.

The front door of our house in Newlands looked out over the fifteen miles to Table Mountain. On clear days one could almost touch it.

Table Mountain, Cape Town 1950

Table Mountain under its cloudy tablecloth!

One day, my mother opened the front door to admire the mountain; then she looked down. There, at her feet, scrawled on a scrap of newspaper that stuck out from under the milk bottles, lay yet another twist of our name. We could never have imagined anything even remotely like it and it had us in stitches. One thing was sure: we were Foreigners, and we had a funny name.

I knew I had a formidable name, an honorable name, even a forbid-able name! I had found *that* out long before when I had tried to offer my services to the neighbors to clean their windows, towards the end of World War II, when I was only five.

That was the time when there was not a single crust of bread when one was hungry; and it was so cold. Feet were wrapped up in newspapers before being stuffed into rubber boots. It was in those days that I found our songbird lying frozen in its cage, and no amount of rattling the heavy bunch of keys could make it get up again.

It was in those days too, that our sausage dog, *Taki,* gobbled up the neighbor's rooster and nearly caused a catastrophe.

That was the time of nerves, when everything was staggering and drove one crazy, absolutely crazy, and the world had gone mad. That was the time when the sirens sent one rushing to the cellar.

So it was not the right time for a hungry little

girl of five to go and tell her Daddy that she had had a perfectly marvelous idea for making a few extra pennies.

"Not *my* daughter!" said my father, going white around the mouth.

One did not trifle with my father, not about cleaning the neighbors' windows, nor about anything else.

Hungarian (*Magyarul*) was the language (*nyelv*) my parents spoke to each other: it was the language of whispers - for that which I was too young to hear. To me they spoke German. But the language of whispers sank into the depths of me, there to remain, unsuspected and unused till, ten years later and on another continent, I got the Red Cross job of distributing clothing to the immigrant Hungarian refugees in 1956.

That was how I learned two languages at once, though not correctly, let alone perfectly. But I was not alone in this. Hadn't I often heard that our German was – quite candidly - *weird!* Who had ever heard of some of the words we used, like *Spagat* for string and *Zecker* for a shopping bag?

Nor did it stop there. By the time I arrived in London - then just nineteen - they told me I must be *brilliant* to speak so many languages. I did not know then that most English spoke only English. I took languages for granted; they were simply a fact of life: when my father said, "Time to leave," I soon found myself in another foreign place, on the threshold of another door, reciting my formidable name, together with the standard opening that began with: "I speak no..."

Back then, languages lined up to claim me. French and Arabic were next on the list in Mataria, Cairo, where our uncle and aunt resided and welcomed us in their home. It was in Egypt that I rode my first camel, bumpily, to the pyramids, and begged to be let down again; and visited the Aqsunqur Mosque, (The Blue Mosque, 1347) in the heart of Cairo, after washing my feet.

It was there, in Cairo, that I stood on the brink of my new classroom and recited my name and the new phrase in which I had been drilled: *"Je ne parle pas Français!"* To which some gawking girls replied, *"Kwoah?"*

It was in Cairo, too, that I underwent my first lesson in the new language - English. Oh! That preposterous, definite article: *The!*

No one who has never experienced the problem could possibly imagine what that tiny English word does to a foreigner the first time it hits him. Innocently the class teacher chalks it up on the blackboard in large letters, then turns to look at the class expectantly, while Egyptian throats try, in vain, to pronounce it. *De... ddd - dd - de?*

Nipped tongues spit out that dreaded word against angry teeth that try, in vain, to snap it between them.

Perhaps it was this Anglo-Saxon invasion into the heart of Egypt that caused those widespread throated longings that spread to my lunch-tin. My foreigner's sandwiches, though made by my aunt's turbaned Arab waiter, were prematurely ambushed and devoured by break-time, and I'd find my lunch-tin emptied, even of its knife and fork.

Our plump Nanny, *Regine*, took this very much to heart. So every morning she would slip into my hand, in the greatest secrecy, one *Millième* for bubble gum. (Today one might think of it as a penny). My father had most strictly forbidden it. Not even one? I had asked. No, he had snapped. Bubble-gum has germs!

One Millième King Farouk (1947)

(I discovered this Egyptian 1947 coin of 1 *Millième* bearing the head of King Farouk on the internet. Ten *Millièmes* made one Piaster and 100 *Piasters* made one pound).

And so I would wander off to the school

tuck shop with my illicit *Millième*, and emerge triumphantly to blow pink bubbles.

Almost every afternoon I would return home equipped with my new tongue-twisting English word and an empty lunch tin, but having had fun with my bubble-gum. I kept Regine's secret, and she kept mine. Until the fateful day we were found out...

What I loved most about Regine was that she could read coffee cups. She would make thick Turkish coffee, pour it into a tiny cup - half full only - drink a few sips and then turn the cup upside down. Then she would wait while the coffee grounds settled into patterns around the inside of the cup. After a while she would turn the cup around, pick it up, and gaze into its mysterious patterns with her deep, dark eyes, for a long while.

When I turned nine, I wanted to find out for myself what my future might hold. What was in store for me? So I would try to read coffee cups, just like Regine. I would sneak into the kitchen when it was empty, drain the last coffee out of the pot, take a sip - just to make sure I had got the ritual right - and then pitch out the ghastly stuff. Then I'd turn the cup upside down and would wait in silent awe, while the gods deliberated on my fate. Then, when the moment had ripened, I, too, would straighten the cup once more, pore over it for a long time, sigh deeply, and gaze at the mountains and valleys of my future.

By the end of that year in Cairo, I could speak French and Arabic. But as we moved on, these new languages were of no further use to me. My one asset: the ability to say *The!*

Regine had seen travel in the patterns of my future. The grinds of the coffee cup had spoken true. Soon a ship was to take us into the waters of the future. Durban, a new port lay ahead. Our new country was South Africa, the country that offered my father a job. It could have been South America - and then my set of new languages would have been different. Now it was English and Afrikaans, with Latin soon to be thrown in.

My father sent us to the Drakensberg Mountains in Natal (renamed KwaZulu-Natal in 1994) till he was ready to send for us. Thus we found ourselves in a new dream.

In the foothills of the scenic southern Drakensberg mountains (now part of the uKhahlamba World Heritage site), lies the charming Drakensberg Gardens Hotel. I loved it there. Passionately! It had everything a little girl could dream of. There was Jim at the hotel. He was about fifty. He was always around, and his job was to make sure everyone was happy.

Breakfasts were a delight; for us, such great choice was amazing. But what I loved most was the crunchy grilled cheese toasts that went by the name of Welsh rarebit.

It was made with butter or margarine; all-purpose flour; light or dark beer; shredded sharp Cheddar cheese; a little salt; dry mustard, paprika, pepper and Worcestershire sauce.

One day I had nine "second" helpings. And to this day I believe there is nowhere on earth where Welsh rarebit is made as well as at the Drakensberg Garden Hotel!

There were horses, too, and mountain rides. It was Jim who accompanied the longer horse riding hikes.

In the nearby hillside, there was a big cave, and other children to play with. They let me join them, and taught me how to light a fire; we even had a kettle to boil over a tripod in that Drakensberg cave. But what I loved most was that the children had a secret.

One day they decided to trust me with it - on condition I would never, *ever*, tell a grown-up.

There was an old lady at the hotel, bedecked and bejeweled and heavily made up. Her room opened into the garden, and I would see her sitting on her porch every afternoon. Folds of skin on her neck hung wrinkled under her crop like that of a turkey. She kept them rolled up with a velvet choker, studded with a large jewel just above her Adam's apple. At first I walked past her warily. Then I went a little closer. One day I tiptoed right up to her.

"Do you know," I whispered, "there are fairies in the caves. We leave them biscuits on tiny plates and water in doll's cups. And the next morning it is gone."

She looked at me thoughtfully, and slowly a

smile spread over her crinkled face. Then her husky words floated out of her ancient throat, past thickly smeared red lips, to the little girl anxiously waiting, "Oh!, really?"

But something was lost for the telling of that secret.

The holidays drew to a close, the children had to leave, and though I often went back to the cave thereafter, the fairies never returned.

My mother and I remained in the Drakensberg for three months, and I could eat as much as I wanted. These months were a kind interlude between the troubles we had left behind and the challenges we would shortly have to face.

As I grew up, my mother's lament remained with me, echoing from time to time:

"Kyriakos has no vegetables!"

It is only now that I begin to get a glimmering of what she might have meant!!

Our final move had been too challenging. My mother had had to leave everything behind: her Church, her home, her parents, her brother, her sister and all her friends.

And now in Cape Town not even the vegetables were as fresh!

My Mother's Moments

We reached Cape Town just before the Apartheid laws of 1948 were laid down. After Cairo and Durban, it was our third port of call since we had left Europe. There was much that was new in the Cape: the vast expanse of sky, the unforgettable sunsets, and the stars that were so bright in the black dome of night. The distances were great and the roads were long.

Ford Fairlaine

It took forty minutes to walk from the nearest railway station to our house. The big silver car was my father's only extravagance and his pride. He drove with quiet, peaceful assurance, and I always felt safe with him.

"*Goh slauwoo!*" my mother would shout out from the back seat as the car approached a bend, while her arm dropped on the passenger beside her like the gate bar at a railroad crossing.

In her new country Mother set to with a will; she learned to sew by unpicking old blouses and using these as a model for cutting out material. Later she became a nursing aide. "It will help pay the cat's food."

But mother not only settled for an original version of English, she also began to learn the rudiments of the second language, Afrikaans. Soon she felt ready to branch out. One day, on the train back from Sea Point, where she loved to float on the waves, three Afrikaans schoolgirls got on and in heated discussion came to sit opposite her. Mother felt ready to try out her new skills. Presently they sought her opinion. She listened attentively till they got to the question mark.

"*Ja,*" she said, nodding her head.

The girls' discussion grew in fervor. Again they looked to my mother.

"*Jaa,*" she said again, enjoying her success.

Heads close, the girls conferred. Then they turned to my mother once more.

"*Jaaa!*" she repeated vigorously, with a

gesture of the utmost approval.

A shocked silence ensued. Faces turned red; pandemonium broke out. Eyebrows were raised; doubtful fingers pointed at her. But quick as lightning, my mother was back.

"Nee, Nee, Nee!" she exclaimed with a great frown, shaking her head vehemently.

"Ach so!"

Mother saw their smiles broaden as the girls relaxed and then got out at the next stop.

"But that was not the only train journey I remember," she told me with a grin. "One day, when I was still a young woman, I was on my way to London and alone in the compartment. Well, a man got in..."

"A man?"

"Yes," she said, "and he did *not* have good intentions. As we approached the tunnel, he leant towards me, and then, in the dark, his hand..."

"Oh, really! And what did *you* do next?"

"I kept him spellbound with exciting stories."

"And what did *he* do next?"

"Oh! He was absolutely riveted, and forgot his hand in mid-air. But we were out of the tunnel by then."

"Mama, I just can't believe this! Riveted you say?"

"Quite so!"

"Whatever did you tell him?"

"I told him all there was to tell about the

Priest, the Pope and the nuns, every single one of them, all through my convent school years."

"And what happened next?"

"He began to yawn and got out at the next station."

But Mother had yet to attain her greatest glory. One day, she announced that she would learn to drive. She found herself a good South African driving-instructor, Mr. Piet Van der Merwe, and they got on very well. Mother loved the sea, and readily induced him to head in that direction.

"We've been to Sea Point today," she announced triumphantly on their return. "All of the twenty miles. I drove some of the way myself. But come to the car and see what we brought back."

The harassed instructor smiled weakly, opened the trunk, plunged his head and shoulders inside and groped around till he clutched at something. Then he emerged, brought the thing in through the back door and dropped it on the kitchen floor: a red-orange and white creature with long, thick, spiny antennae, horns above its eyes, ten legs and a short, fat tail. I backed away as this large marine Decapoda Reptantia steered in my direction.

"Go and catch it!" Mother commanded, and the man did as he was told. "And bring the creature here, while I bring water to a boil."

Meekly Van der Merwe obeyed.

"You'd better stay for dinner," she added, "now that the food is so fresh!"

Very pleased with herself, my mother stood over the man as he crawled around the kitchen after the spiny lobster, that was making a raspy sound in an attempt to repel his predator!

Then, like the witches of old, she popped it into the boiling cauldron. But when the lobster began to scream, I fled.

My mother took her time learning to drive, making leisurely progress. When she had taken innumerable lessons (I used to think it was about sixty), her instructor mildly suggested: "We should be ending now."

"But you can't do that! Not before I've passed my test."

Mr. Van der Merwe hesitated; he thought hard. Then at last: "I don't think you are quite ready."

"Oh! But it's just a matter of a few more lessons," she insisted.

"Lady, I don't think you will *ever* be ready!"

Piet sighed dolefully.

"Nonsense, my dear," said Mother in dulcet tones. "All I need to do is to practice my parking."

The instructor stood his ground. "In all good conscience I cannot let you take the test."

My mother felt the impact; held him hostage.

"You don't need to worry, my dear," she purred, certain now of victory. "You certainly don't, I can assure you! You can let me take this test with a clear conscience. For you see, all I really want to do is to drive in and out of our garden!"

Piet Van der Merwe tasted freedom; the long night was ending.

Their last ride lay ahead.

A week later he put her through the test himself: and passed her!

My mother got her driving license and began to drive - everywhere.

Riding with her, I was petrified.

SOMEONE WHO CARED

That year, 1956, the long Christmas break was a very special moment. I was out of boarding school - forever. Sixteen, and free! Prepared for everything, but Life!

"The Hungarian immigrants will be arriving in Vanderbijlpark (South Africa) next week. The Red Cross needs a volunteer to distribute clothes. Would the job interest you?" the Roman Catholic priest asked, all in a kafuffle.

He knew my parents spoke several languages, among them Hungarian, and no doubt he hoped I did, too.

The prospect delighted me. I had just passed my Matriculation exams and life held limitless possibilities. I even had a new bicycle! Distances were great, and buses few. My father needed the car to get to work, and most of the time we walked. Thus I became the proud owner of a rapid, rigid, reliable, high-gloss black enamel Ladies loop frame Raleigh Roadster, "The All Steel Bicycle" with a front mirror and a strong rear carrier. It was made of the best British steel: majestic, solid and dependable and built to last a hundred years.

For four and a half decades Hungary had been a closed country. Then the revolt broke out. On 23rd October 1956 a crowd of 23,000 mostly unarmed students took to the streets of Budapest, in spirited but peaceful protest against the government. For 18 days, millions of men, women and children participated, demanding more freedom of speech, trade unions and self-management of the workplace, as well as the release of political prisoners.

We, too, had been immigrants and until recently, had been living in Cape Town. By 1956 we had been in South Africa for eight years. Just two years previously my father, a mechanical engineer, had obtained a position in Vanderbijlpark, in the Transvaal, designing mine winders to meet South Africa's deep level mining requirements. It was a cordial workplace, with kind people. The Managing Director of the engineering company was an Afrikaner whose ancestors had been in South Africa for centuries and whose wife was the most hospitable and courteous lady I had ever met. My father's immediate superior was German; his draughtsman, British. In this environment my father was appreciated, and so were we.

It was here that we became members of a community; indeed, we became citizens. My father maintained lifelong gratitude to South Africa. "This country took us in, and gave me work. It enabled us to start a new life. Now it is my country."

We had heard the disappointing news that the Hungarian Revolution had failed and mass exodus had begun. Over 200,000 Hungarians had fled to Austria. The number of refugees became almost unmanageable. The Austrian Minister of the Interior had to ask for international help. It had become urgent for the refugees to move on. There had been a world-wide response.

Fifty years later, on 10th October 2006, the UNHCR news reviewed it and reported:

"The relief and resettlement operations that followed were quite extraordinary - 100,000 people were resettled out of Austria in the first 10 weeks alone. In all, 37 countries spanning five continents took in resettled Hungarians in an unprecedented wave of international solidarity on behalf of refugees."

The largest numbers emigrated to the United States and Canada. Israel was prepared to admit every Hungarian Jewish refugee in Austria.

South Africa offered to accept 1,000 refugees, 500 carefully picked artisans with their families, and 500 dependants on humanitarian grounds. The first contingent of 75 (which included selected workers, their wives and children, and 8 men to be trained as miners) arrived on the 18th December 1956; the second party (among them 23 children, the youngest being six months old) was due on the 21st; the third batch on Christmas Eve, the fourth group was expected on January 2nd. They had lost their homes and some of them nearly their lives. They arrived very tired, but free. Only three of the first group spoke English. But the gratitude of the immigrants lay in their eyes: "Thank You, South Africa." Through Mr. J. Jankovics, a Hungarian who had lived in S.A. for some time, and acted as their liaison officer, the immigrants promised, "We'll prove worthy of your trust." (*The Star*, 22.12.1956).

Many Hungarians were at the airport to welcome and cheer their fellow countrymen as the first group of refugees came off the Skymaster of the Flying Tiger Line.

Vanderbijlpark (VDBP) was a small new industrial town about thirty-nine miles south of Johannesburg. It had only been proclaimed a town in 1949 and attained municipal status in 1952. By 1956 it was able to provide two modern well-designed and comfortable workers' hostels as a temporary reception centre for the refugees.

One evening, with mischief in his eyes, my otherwise very serious father said, "I will teach you the Hungarian alphabet."

And began right away.

My father did his best to encourage me, but my attempts at Hungarian pronunciation had him in stitches. Hard as I tried to imitate the sounds he made, I could hardly get my tongue around them. The double consonants made the situation worse. I distorted them this way and that, till we were doubled up with laughter, and tears ran down our faces. It was the best language lesson I had ever had.

"Once you know the Hungarian alphabet," he assured me, "you can also read."

He taught me the basic vocabulary: Hello or good day (*jó napot kívánok*); yes (*igen*); no (*nem*); thank you (*kösnönöm szépen*), and individual items of clothing. So by the time things got under way, I had learned the essential words, among them *munka*, work.

I loved my job of distributing clothing to the Hungarians: Trousers? Shirt? Shoes?

"*Csinos lány*," I'd hear people say, with *ny* as in *nyet!*

"Papa, what does *csinos lány* mean?" I asked when I got home.

"*Who's* been calling you *that*?" he growled, without explanation. I thought it must be something really bad and forgot to mention it was mainly the men! It took me a while to find that it meant I was *quite a girl!*

I loved this, my first growing-up job. Here I was treated as a responsible adult. How different from the "keep quiet and do as you're told" atmosphere at boarding school.

Many of the donated clothes were brand new. One day my supervisor, Mrs. Van Niekerk, said, "As you are not being paid, I suggest you take a few nice clothes. I myself am not in need of any."

But I certainly was! It takes a long time for immigrant families to catch up. I rummaged through the heaps and piles, and found a pale blue cotton dress that made me feel a million dollars. It was my first really beautiful dress.

People from all over South Africa sent clothing and Christmas gifts. 300 resident Hungarians from Johannesburg and the Reef (many of whom had escaped after WWII and sought refuge in South Africa) came to give the refugees the traditional Christmas turkey dinner. It was they who received their stories of horror. Afterwards they all sang the Hungarian national anthem, and a Hungarian carol.

The Star reported: "Despite memories of terror, they had a merry Christmas." (26 December, 1956)

But the Hungarians were happy for another reason, too - they were smartly turned out. "Gone were the old tattered clothes they had worn when they crossed the frontier into Austria. The women wore summer dresses given by the people of Vanderbijlpark and by the Red Cross in Johannesburg."

The refugees expressed their desire not to become a burden to society, and hoped to be able to start work soon, and indeed, work opportunities arose with surprising rapidity.

One man, an electrician, actually began work on the day after arrival. By the 27th December, twenty refugees were being considered for jobs in the local steel works, eight were taken on by the South African Railways, and nine went to the mines. Hungarian craftsmen, well-trained in at least two or three skilled crafts, are highly regarded artisans, known to work hard and well. As more of them arrived, South African businessmen and industrialists by the hundreds were offering jobs. Even though our streets were not, after all, "lined with gold," the immigrants were "dazzled by big pay prospects" (*The Star*, 19.12.1956). Used to measuring everything they see and want in weeks of pay, and having to save for months or even a year for a suit, the standard of living truly amazed them.

One day I received a call to go to a certain men's outfitters. The proprietor, who spoke little English, told me he had a job for a man named Zsidó (*Zs* as in azure). I was to find him, and to bring him to the shop.

Enthusiastically I set about this new task, cycled to the reception centre and found the Hungarians assembled in the large hall, sitting on the floor after a meeting: quiet, forlorn, homesick, and uncertain about the future.

"Mr. Zsidó?" I called out. "Is there a Mr. Zsidó here? *Munka*! Work!"

A wave of discomfort traveled through the group: shoulders drooped, eyes lowered to stare at the floor; hushed silence, broken only by an awkward cough.

"Mr. Zsidó?" I called out again, never doubting that I had got his name right.

With extreme reluctance, a tall man rose.

Follow me, I beckoned as I led this man, by far taller and much heavier than I, to my sturdy black Raleigh bicycle; solid and dependable. *And sit here* I indicated, pointing to the strong rear carrier.

The man looked at me with the utmost alarm. I tried to reassure him.

"Munka!" I repeated. "You-me-work!"

Petrified, the once brave and freedom-loving man straddled my bicycle carrier, doubtful as to whether this was safer than the revolution he had just escaped. He clasped me tightly, and held on for dear life as I wobbled away with his enormous weight behind me. From time to time a little groan escaped the unhappy creature. Slowly I found my balance and pedaled hard along the *Veld* for the next ten minutes.

Puffing and panting, then flying down an innocent hill while my terrified rider tightened his embrace, I reached the outfitters with my pale passenger, who edged himself off the carrier and unfurled his full height.

The proprietor awaited us in front of his shop.

"I found Mr. Zsidó!" I called out triumphantly.

With a burst of smiles, a stream of Hungarian and much gesticulation, the beaming proprietor met his fellow countryman, and offered him a job.

Overwhelmed by such a welcome, and with the prospect of security the Hungarian, now safely off my bicycle carrier, turned to me with a gentle smile. "My name is Tibor Lakatos," he said.

"You're *not* Mr. Zsidó?" I stuttered, completely taken aback.

"No, but I am indeed a z*sidó* - a Jew!"

From then on my parents often invited the immigrants to our modest little home and they'd spill out from the living-room onto the stoep. Most of them were men. Among them was *Sándor* an upholsterer, a small man whom my father hired to turn the upholstery of the settee and two armchairs in our living room inside out, hoping the reverse side of the material would look less worn. He and his wife had two dear little children and they set up home in a garage, free of charge. One single woman was a very experienced dressmaker. Another worker, skilled in making chicken wire fencing, set to work making huge rolls of that. I met one young woman, a gymnast, who had been to many operas in Hungary, while I had been to none. She got a job in a stocking factory, working alongside Black women. István, "a leader in Budapest [who had been] too busy fighting," and Margit, finally found time to get married. Now that the revolution was over!

The sister of a college friend had married one of the 1956 Hungarian immigrants to South Africa. This gave me the opportunity to enquire about his first impressions. His wife replied: "When Miklós came to South Africa he was sixteen and so went to school to do Standards 9 and 10. He doesn't remember much about how he was received in Vanderbijlpark, except that the food was very strange. He remembers eating *Boerewors* (farmers' sausage) for the first time and finding it very sweet compared to the Hungarian sausage *(Kolbász)*. The hardest thing for him was the language - it took him about six months to learn some English. He found the African people very friendly, although he had never seen any before."

As a young man Miklós began to work by winding thread onto reels of cotton. Later he established his own business, which is still flourishing today.

One of the people who helped the immigrants in her own quiet way, was a very gracious, unassuming, elderly lady. Goodness and kindness radiated from her. She took the bus from Vereeniging (ten miles away) and would spend most of the day with the refugees, bringing them cheer and encouragement. She came often, and I wondered who she was.

Late one afternoon, this lady joined us in the Red Cross space. "You are doing a fine job," she said to my supervisor, Mrs. Van Niekerk. "The Hungarians told me you have been looking after them splendidly."

"Would you like to have a cup of tea with us?" my supervisor asked the elderly lady.

"I'd love to," she replied.

But as she looked at her watch, her face clouded. "I am supposed to be in Johannesburg this evening for a meeting. But the last bus leaves in twenty minutes. I absolutely *must* catch it."

Mrs. Van Niekerk looked most uncomfortable. "I would offer to drive you myself," she said, "but my husband has taken our car for the day."

"Never mind," I said. "We'll call a taxi."

The cab phone rang and rang, but all in vain. Neither of the two local taxis was available.

"What am I to do? I *must* be there this evening," she said, getting desperate.

"It's not too late yet. I'll phone the Church. There's bound to be someone around who could drive you."

The phone rang and rang, but no one answered, and time was slipping away.

"Well, perhaps you could hitch-hike," I suggested cheerfully. The elderly lady agreed at once. But as we stood at the side of the road, not a single car passed. And the minutes went ticking by.

Just as the situation seemed completely hopeless, my eyes caught the glint of shiny the black Raleigh Roadster, made of the best British steel, solid and dependable, and built to last a hundred years.

"I could take you to the station myself," I said, pointing to my royal steed.

My supervisor looked up to the Heavens, tried to say something, swallowed it, and turned pale.

"That would be wonderful!" the lady replied. Without a moment's hesitation, and with infinite grace, she settled herself on the rear carrier side-saddle, and laced her arms around my waist.

So there we were, the lady and I: she a silvery seventy and I sixteen, with twelve minutes and several miles between us and the last long-distance bus to Johannesburg. I pedaled for all I was worth. She felt as light as a feather and my sturdy steed responded gallantly. Suddenly from behind me, came a delighted, tinkling laugh. Her gaiety was infectious and the harder I pedaled, the more we laughed. We reached the bus station with two minutes to spare. Immensely relieved, and looking at least thirty years younger, she waved cheerfully as the bus drove off.

Back at the hostel, my supervisor was waiting for me, as anxious as before.

"I got the lady to the bus in time," I announced.

Mrs. Van Niekerk heaved a sigh of relief.

"But who *is* she?" I asked.

Her reply came in hushed, respectful tones:

"A countess!" she said. "She is the Countess Jankovics!"

The year 2006 marked the 50th anniversary of the 1956 Hungarian Revolution, and on the 23rd October Hungarians throughout the world celebrated.

I needed to consult the South African newspaper archives, and in spite of their busy schedule, two kind, efficient ladies offered their help and sent me more than 22 articles each from the Johannesburg University archives (*The Star, The Rand Daily Mail*) and from Cape Town, (*The Cape Times, The Cape Argus* and *Die Burger*) and the South African Red Cross National Office. However, in spite of the fine journalism provided by the press at the time, it has been impossible in a short story about a moment in history and a flash in a young girl's life, to do justice to all the information received.

South Africans responded generously. Hungary's "plight moved people in all walks of life and of all ages to give what they can." It was Nurses who started the ball rolling by giving £120 to the Red Cross. The 300 strong Hungarian Community in Johannesburg collected £2,000. Eighty employees of an engineering firm decided to donate their overtime pay to the Red Cross Street collections that were held in Cape Town. In addition, there was a Gala concert, an open-air party, a fashion show, and a young child emptied her piggy bank. "Money for the Hungarian Relief Fund organized by the Red Cross continues to come in at Cape Town in a steady stream, and by yesterday the total had reached £13,100 16s. 5d, an increase of more than £1,000 since Saturday." (Cape Times, December 12, 1956). Of this, £40,000 had already been sent to the Headquarters of the Red Cross in Geneva.

The effort required in the Cape had to go far beyond the initial 1,000. But more and more was asked of them as several Norwegian and Italian ships bearing large numbers of Hungarian immigrants on their way to Australia, called at Table Bay. By January 22, 1957 the total number of refugees to have called was nearly 1,500. Another 855 were expected. The *Cape Times* reported that "The Cape Town branch of the South African Red Cross Society took a three-ton load of clothing, shoes and toilet requirements given by the public of Cape Town for the refugees, to the quayside soon after the liner had docked (…) to be distributed at sea."

By the time three ships had been equipped, Cape Town was running short of stocks. 12,000 more refugees were to call at the City on four following ships. Another appeal was made. Individual creativity came into play. One couple organized a clothing collection in Paarl and Malmesbury. On January 27, 1957 they brought some truly beautiful clothes in a very large box to the quayside. Someone had even given evening dresses that still had their price tag on, and "a Cinderella dream came true for two pretty Hungarian refugee girls (of 15 and 17)."

HOW TO BUY A PIG

Following the Second World War, a generation of Europeans was uprooted. Families were split; some members left; some remained behind. But on both sides of the divide there were those who cherished memories of long ago, of the time that came before - before it all changed. Looking back, it seems almost like a fairy-tale. A relative, now eighty-five, related an experience in her youth.

Once upon a time there was a beautiful young lady called Teri, who lived in a land that had once been part of the Austro-Hungarian Empire. But that was before parts of it were chopped off; and a new regime came into power.

Teri belonged to a large family. Her maternal Grandfather and Grandmother did not live very far away, and her mother often sent her children to visit them. Grandfather was a landowner and manufactured agricultural machines in his own factory. He was the Patriarch of the family, and in society, an important man. He had a son who, likewise, became an important person in time and liked to go riding in the Royal Hunting Forest on the outskirts of town. The Royal Hunting Forest was abundant with game. Deer with their fawns, and dark brown wild boars with their reddish brown yellow-striped young, ran free. It was a wonderful green wood of seven hundred and forty hectares with tall, ancient oak trees and a little stream that ran through it.

Many different species of birds celebrated springtime in this wood. The woodpecker chiseled his nesting cavity in dry trees and loudly pecked the resonant trunks. The notes of the nightingale rang sweet and clear through the forest. Pheasants, too, were plentiful. But the iridescent Gold, Silver and Diamond Pheasants were bred specially for Royal privilege and pleasure.

Towards nightfall, one could even get a glimpse of the now almost extinct rubbery black fire salamanders with their orange blotches or stripes, like little flames between logs on the cool, damp forest floor.

Grandfather's house was not far from the Royal Hunting Forest and Teri's house not far from his. She grew up healthy, strong and became lovelier with the years. Young men looked at her admiringly.

One day her mother sent Teri to the grandparents with a freshly baked cake. When she arrived, her grandfather studied her long, and with a certain satisfaction. He seemed to notice for the first time that his granddaughter was nearly grown up; soon a young man would come to claim her. It struck him that the time for this had come much sooner than he had anticipated. Grandfather had long since given her his blessing for such an eventuality.

"You may marry whom you like," he had said to her, "rich or poor, educated or not, handsome or not."

The day Teri turned eighteen, Grandfather said,

"Now there is only one thing still missing from your education."

"What have you in mind, Grandfather?"

"Look, you are fully grown now. Soon you will want to get married. You'll have a family and have to manage a household. And you will also have to slaughter pigs. So there is something you still have to learn."

"And what is that?" she asked with trusting expectancy.

"How to buy a pig. No one can get married without knowing that!"

(In some ancient cultures, the pig was sacred and was sacrificed to the gods. It was the symbol of fertility, wealth and good fortune. To possess a pig meant one was well-stocked. No doubt Grandfather knew that!)

"Who is going to come to the market with me?" asked Teri, somewhat taken aback.

"No one! You will have to go alone!"

"But Grandfather, you can't mean *me*. Do

please send my brothers."

Grandfather was a kind man, but he meant what he said, and that was that!

"But I don't know the first thing about buying pigs. And anyway, I am not going alone!"

"*Muszáj,*" said Grandfather. Which meant, *You have to!* "To try is to learn," he continued, and with this he convinced her, for Teri enjoyed learning.

Then he gave her detailed instructions.

"The pig must weigh more than a hundred kilos. Its color must be light; its coat smooth and not curly. And, you must bring a perfectly healthy pig back home."

Had Grandfather taken leave of his senses?

"But a pig costs a lot of money," she objected. "And if the pig I buy is not the right one, then you are going to be angry with me. What if I choose a pig that is too expensive, or even sick? I've never bought a pig before. That's not something one learns at piano lessons!"

"No one will blame you if something goes wrong," he said kindly. "I am only sending you off to learn. Go and give it a try. That's all."

At last came the Saturday of the December animal market, which took place on a large square, in deep winter snow. Teri left the house early, feeling very alone. There were a great many peasants, some on their own, some with their wives. And there were so many animals; not only pigs, but also goats, sheep, horses, cattle and poultry. The pigs grunted, the horses neighed and snorted, sheep and goats bleated, cocks crowed and cows lowed. Each made itself heard in its own way. Some of the peasants had also brought their dogs; these joined the fray. The peasants tried to make themselves heard above the din.

Teri began to look for a pig, just like Grandfather had told her to do. But there were masses of pigs; stout, heavy-bodied ones, pink, white and black, some with piglets. They romped around so much, that some of their curly tails nearly got intertwined. She had never seen so many pigs in one place. How could she possibly find the right one? She tried to look on the bright side of things: at least the sun is shining now, she consoled herself.

Every peasant wanted to sell his animals first; everyone wanted to be heard; some took to shouting. They bargained this way and that; some prices fell. Here a horse was sold; there, some sheep. Then a cow was led away. People and animals shoved in all directions.

Teri wanted to fulfill her Grandfather's wishes down to the last detail, but as she examined one pig after the other, she got confused. There was such a muddle! The pigs were boisterous, and the peasants shoved them this way and that. Some pigs had a curly tail, although their coats were straight. As the day progressed, the snow became spotted. Most of the pigs were clean; but Teri noticed that some had dirty feet. And that made her think about her own feet.

"Something's not right," she thought, looking at her wet shoes. Only now did she realize how cold her feet had become and how cold she felt.

"I can*not* choose," she said to herself. "I do *not* have to buy a pig! It takes a man to come up with an idea like that! That's not something one should expect of a girl."

Revolt brewed up in her.

(The brothers were pretty pleased to have escaped this whole business.)

"I don't know how to find my way round all this," she thought. "And anyway, how could I? I can cook, paint and play the piano. I can knit, sew and am good at handicrafts. I can even play the organ in church. But to buy a pig! That's something I can't do! And to be tested and taught – that's something I don't want! Enough is enough!"

So she decided to go back home to get help. "I'll ask someone to come with me," she said to herself. "That still leaves me free to make the final decision myself."

But as she turned her back on the pigs and turned wistfully towards home, a sudden inspiration stopped her; a solution dawned. She calmed down and began to smile.

The country lads could not take their eyes

off the pretty young lady and wondered what she was doing at the animal market. Some of the men ragged her, a little.

"Hey you, young lady! You have such beautiful eyes!"

But Teri heard nothing and saw no one. Her whole body had become a single eye focused on the pig market. She began to have fun. Her confidence grew: now she knew she would succeed. She noticed that some farmers had brought five pigs, some two, others only one.

Teri forgot her wet shoes; forgot her cold feet. Her confidence grew; yes, she *could* do this by herself. Soon she would have the right pig, and Grandfather would be very pleased.

Then, with the glow of certainty Teri made her choice. She had found the right pig, the one and only - a clean, pot-bellied, straight-haired, smooth pink pig.

"I have only one question," she said to the peasant to whom the pig belonged.

"Yes, Milady?"

"What does your pig weigh?"

"One hundred and fifteen kilos," the man answered proudly. "I fed it the finest grains every day."

"That's great!" said Teri. "I want to buy *your pig* for my grandfather."

By midday the deal was done. The amiable farmer lifted the pig onto the back of his cart, helped Teri up and drove her home.

She rode the coach like a princess; the horse in front, the pig at the back.

Illustration © *Gaby*

In Grandfather's villa the family waited, tense with excitement. When the horse-cart arrived, they all rushed out to the yard: Grandfather and Grandmother, her father and mother, and all her siblings. They encircled the cart and admired the pink pig. Teri descended from the high seat like a heroine returning from a great adventure, and was given a royal welcome.

Grandfather said, "I am so proud of you!"

The peasant lifted the pig out of the cart, and it charged around the yard on its short legs. The two men got on well. The pig was exactly what Grandfather had asked for: a clean, pot-bellied, straight-haired, pink pig in excellent health. Grandfather paid the peasant's price without attempting to bargain. Teri thanked the man who had driven her home so courteously. Happy and satisfied, the peasant drove off.

"Congratulations!" said Grandfather and gave Teri a bear hug. "But tell me, how did you manage to buy the right pig?"

Teri's eyes sparkled.

"I didn't buy a pig at all. In fact," she said, "In fact, I wasn't even looking for a pig!"

"What on earth do you mean?"

"Well you see, while I was standing there cold, and feeling perfectly miserable, I had a sudden idea. Instead of looking for a beautiful, healthy pig, I would look for a peasant with clean, well-polished boots. For a man who polishes his boots, is also a man who looks after his pig. And such a pig cannot possibly turn out to be sick. And this man's black leather boots shone like a mirror!"

Teri's brothers and sister were full of admiration. "I would never have got such an idea," said the one. "I just knew you could do it," said the other.

Everyone was happy and pleased with her purchase. And also with her!

Grandfather smiled and said,
"Now you are ready to get married."

GREEK HOSPITALITY

2 7th August 2007: Greece is burning. 170 fires erupt simultaneously from the Ionian Sea in the west, Ioannina in the north and the Peloponnese in the south. Fed by gale force winds, walls of flame descend on houses and villages. The land of sun and light, dreams, hopes and illusions, is going up in smoke. Two months later, on 9th September, Theodorous N. Ikonomou, the President of the Greek Forest Owners Association, reported that "for four days repeatedly over 200 fires occurred per 24 hours. Over 150 arson mechanisms were collected in the aftermath of the fires. 75 human lives were lost, including five fire-fighters. There was relatively little damage to ancient monuments but considerably more to Byzantine churches and other treasured buildings."

Greece is burning: I am outraged. The fires burn through my decades and awaken youthful memories; youthful passion; youthful love.

Many years ago, in 1961, Pamela, my best friend from South African schooldays, was sharing a flat with me in London. Then, wanting to go on a tour of Europe, she invited me to join her and Maureen, another South African, on the trip to Italy and Greece. I was about to turn 21, and like the three little maids from school, we were ripe for adventure.

I knew almost nothing about Greece, save that it was full of islands and monuments, but by the age of ten, I had met a live Greek, Mr. Kyriakos, the vegetable vendor in Cape Town. So I knew: Greeks sell vegetables!

At twenty, in London, I then met a Greek girl, Jota, a goddess if ever there was one, and whenever she got mad at her boyfriend, an engineer twice her age, she would unfailingly threaten, "*Aiee* come with the *kitshennaiff*!" A few minutes after threatening to come after him with the kitchen knife, she would be smiling in all innocence – having forgotten all about it. Jota had him completely bewitched! As indeed all of her admirers!

So I also learned that Greek goddesses were passionate and temperamental. Now, Jota also knew, by first name, all the *shipónas* – the flamboyant clan of Greek shipowners who met each year at the Cathedral of the Divine Wisdom (Saint Sophia) in London.

Jota said, "If you come to Church with me this Greek Orthodox Easter, you will see all the *shipónas*. Come, and they will invite us to their homes. Easter is the greatest time for feasting and celebration." She went on to relate that people begin to gather in the church by eleven p.m., many carrying large white candles. The church bell tolls at midnight as the priests announce *Christ is Risen*! There are fireworks and even gunshots from the crowd as each person answers with the joyous responses – Truly He is Risen and *Alithinós O Kírios* – True is the Lord. Where after the people carry their candles to their homes, and let them burn all night, to symbolize the return of Light to the world; then the feasting begins. The traditional foods on the Resurrection Table are smoked salted pork, cheeses; creamy, lemony soup made from the lamb sweetmeats; and Greek Easter breads. Plenty of wine, Retsina and Ouzo insure a feast that will last throughout the night. And yet people are up early on Easter Sunday morning.

Happy Easter!

Slowly I gathered bits of information: even to-day, the Greek fleet is the largest in the world. However, Pamela, who was a year older and wiser, had more profound knowledge. She had read Homer by the age of nine, and knew about Greek hospitality. "It is quite exceptional!" she said, and quoted Menelaus speaking to Telemachus, Odyseus's son: "... far be it from me to keep you here for any length of time, if you wish to get back. (...) What I say, is, treat a man well while he is with you, but let him go when he wishes. However, do give me time to bring you some presents…"

Though we were three in the car all the way through Italy, only two of us assured the driving. I did have a driving license, but almost no practice. My one attempt to relieve my friends was short-lived: as I took the wheel along a dusty country lane and wound my way through herds of goats and sheep, herdsmen and horse carts, it became obvious that my feet seemed altogether unsure which pedal to press, and when: the accelerator, the clutch or the brake? My ten-minute shift came to an abrupt end, and no one (ever) asked me to drive again.

On the way to Rome, "as the sun sank and light thickened on every pathway," we stopped at the Etruscan Necropolis of Banditaccia, a short distance outside the small town of Cerveteri. And it was there, quite by chance, that a vital fragment was added to my pre-Hellenic kaleidoscope. The place was deserted, save for an elderly archaeologist and his rather prim wife, who introduced themselves. Shocked at seeing young girls out so late and hoping to instill some sense into us, the gentleman proposed an itinerary for our intended ten days in Greece. And, to ensure our safety, he issued a stern warning: "The Greeks will try to give you Ouzo! Don't accept it! They are used to it, but you are not. Greece, Yes! But Ouzo, No!"

We saw many wonderful works of art in Italy, such as *David* and the Sistine Chapel, but it was a relief to get away from Italian men of all ages, who pursued us in spite of the most vigorous protest, till we finally had to enquire from an older woman what might be the most effective insult, and resorted to repeating: Go *casa*, go home!

We took the ferry from Brindisi, and after a stress-free crossing, stepped onto Greek soil in Piraeus towards nightfall. A pleasant welcome awaited us at the new Youth Hostel. We were the first to stop there; it had fresh, whitewashed walls, a small kitchen and showers. Our room had four new bunk beds, but as yet no mattresses. We stayed there for the night, grateful for its safety and the courtesy of the Greek caretaker. The next morning we stepped out confident and happy, crisscrossed with the imprint of the wiry whorls of the naked metal springs.

The sun rose. Pamela drove us to Athens and we arrived innocently on a sweltering August day, insouciant as yet of being in Greece without a word of Greek. The heat hung thickly over the city, like a kind of smothering daylight - moon blanket, blocking out the sun.

Just then I was assailed by a desperate need. "Pam, stop here please!"

But there was nowhere to park, and so, swept along by the crazy traffic, Pam headed northwards, till we found ourselves in Kifissia, one of the most exclusive suburbs of Athens.

"I can't wait a moment longer!"

"Hold it," said Pam. "I'm stopping here!"

She parked in front of the imposing five-star Theoxenia Palace Hotel.

"But we can't go in looking like this!"

"Why not?"

A red carpet led up the stairs to the majestic white columns.

Immaculate in her cool drip-dry white Dacron outfit, Pam marched confidently toward the stately portal while, hot and crumpled, Maureen and I tagged along behind her. The previous night had done little for our appearance.

The doorman saw us coming and dashed off to fetch the manageress. A moment later an extremely elegant lady in her thirties came hurrying down the hall. I feared she was going to shoo us away, like something unwanted. But she welcomed us with open arms.

"We were expecting you," she said. "Are you the Royal Ballet?"

"No, but may we use the Ladies?"

Without a hint of surprise, she ushered us with the utmost courtesy through the lily-decked foyer to a luxurious pink marble sanctuary, and left us to it. This was not just a bathroom, but a room to relax in - an invitation to take one's time. We sat on plush velour seats, freshened up in pink marble hand basins, and drank cool water to our hearts' content. When we finally emerged, the staff made no reference to the length of time we had spent there, and treated us with the same courtesy as before.

"You see," said Pam, "*that's* Greek hospitality! Just like in the days of Homer!"

"The hotel is not called *Theoxenia* for nothing," I replied. "One would think we really were royal dignitaries!"

(Almost fifty years later I learned through the internet, that "Theoxenia is a tradition from antiquity – a feast held in honor of a god or gods, to which the deity is invited and served as a special guest. In the Homeric ages, hospitality was under the protection of Zeus, the God of the Gods, who was also attributed with the title of Xenios Zeus (*xenos* means stranger). Hospitality for Ancient Greeks was of the utmost importance. A stranger passing outside a Greek house could be invited inside the house by the family. The host washed the stranger's feet, offered him food and wine and only after he was feeling comfortable could be asked tell his/her name.)"

Refreshed, Pamela drove us back to the centre of Athens and to the Parthenon, a temple built in the 5th Century B.C. for Athena - goddess of war, handicrafts, wisdom and self-realization.

We marveled at the tremendous strength and solidity of this building, at its breathtaking beauty. The marble it is built with has mellowed into the warmest ivory tinged with rose, varying with the sun.

What astounded me, however, was the live frieze of visitors. Most of the women were elegantly dressed in white. Draped against its Doric columns, or silhouetted against this sunlit symbol of antiquity, they stood motionless, while their men, at a respectful distance, gazed worshipfully into their cameras. Were they playing out some primordial ceremony for vestal virgins?

The August heat slowed us down; we stopped rushing around trying to see everything, and instead of the planned ten days, spent two weeks in Greece. Now we headed South in the direction of Sparta. The sun sank.

We stopped at a village, but found that there was nowhere to sleep. However, a paternal policeman shepherded us to the house of some of his local friends. A large matron in black welcomed us into her home and offered us her flat roof, and had her son bring up some mattresses. Then she offered us food and drink, but we had just been lifting lids and sniffing pots in a nearby Taverna, had delighted in fresh vegetables and lamb, and were replete.

The air was warm and friendly. Cozy in our open-air beds, with our torch beside us, we fell asleep under the protective dome of the starry Greek night sky.

Dawn came early, but not with rosy fingers! (Unlike in the Odyssey!) Deep groans startled me out of sleep, only to find Maureen rocking to and fro, nursing a finger. "Something bit me," she said grimly, "a yellow brown thing with four pairs of legs, front claws and a horrible long tail."

Pamela woke up too, but said, "I've been sick all night and can't move. Go and get help."

I ran to fetch the landlady. Alarmed by what Fate had dealt us in her house, she shouted out with all her might: *"Skropio! Skropio!"*

I feared the worst.

Had Maureen's time come? How many hours did she have left?

The call echoed through the house and again and again, we heard the woman's lament: *Skropio! Skropio!* Such a disgrace! Was she not every inch a Greek; one of a race noted for hospitality, today as in Ancient Greece? Was it not her obligation to be hospitable to travelers? Had she not always been proud of inviting to her house a passing stranger?

Her voice held terror. What divine retribution would be hers? She had not washed the feet of the strangers, but with true kindness of heart, had given them beds. And yet, here she was, betrayed by a scorpion.

(Almost fifty years later I learned that the policy of Xenia also includes the protection of travelling bards - and no doubt we, as young girls, must have fallen into this category. Their safety was believed to have been secured by the aegis-wielding Zeus. If one played host to a traveler and performed poorly, one would incur the wrath of a god).

The family came running, their voices resounding like a tragic chorus. They peered into every nook and cranny, scoured every inch of the domain. That scorpion had to be found and boiled. Maureen must drink the liquid! Only thus could the host's honor be restored.

(Wise too late, I discovered on the internet that Andreas, who runs the "End of the World" tavern on Samos, keeps two bottles of Ouzo handy; one is two-thirds full of dead scorpions and one-third amber liquid; the other contains a poisonous viper. "When I catch a live scorpion," he said, "I put it into the bottle of Ouzo; as it drowns it releases its sting into the liquid. This is the perfect antidote for a scorpion sting. Put this liquid on a sting and the pain will instantly disappear.")

But *this* scorpion had made off with its life!

We were advised to hurry to the nearest hospital, some twenty kilometers away.

Maureen began to have cramps. Most deaths, I was to discover, occur during the first 24 hours after the sting. "Scorpions use their pincers to grasp their prey; then they arch their tail over their body to drive the stinger into the prey to inject their venom, sometimes more than once."

Maureen's heart rate shot up! So did mine! What options had they, bar to depend on me? Death by scorpion or death by driving?

Getting my sick friends to the hospital in Corinth was going to be up to me! But would I remember which pedal did what; which foot went where? And be able to get them there in one piece?

Maureen was in no condition to object and was willing to take the risk. Pale and shaky, Pam had no objection either. I felt somewhat ill myself, but at least I knew that, like my cat, I had another six lives left!

My two companions were helped into the car, and with tearful hugs and heartfelt hopes, a crestfallen, tragic cast waved us off.

Feeling heroic, I mastered the fiery engine, negotiated narrow lanes and sharp inclines hoping for the best, and victoriously drove my two friends to the hospital in Corinth without killing them. I explained why we had come, handed over my patients, and booked myself in safely for stomach ills.

Maureen was wheeled off in great haste, while Pamela and I were given beds side by side. I fell asleep. When I woke up, I saw a tall, dark, handsome stranger bending over Pamela, while she gazed up at him with a beatific smile. It was the doctor, examining her with lively attention – a man who obviously had things under control. We shall name him Dr. Lefteris Constantinides.

He said he had identified the creature that had stung Maureen.

"The *Mesobuthus gibbosus* is the most potent scorpion in Europe. It can inflict much pain -

but that is all. So your friend will soon be all right."

Dr. Constantinides cast a cursory glance in my direction, diagnosed Pam and me as having "too-much-travel sickness" and had us put on black tea, toast and rest. Whereupon he left...

Only to return at midday with two companions to whom he introduced us: Dr. Manolis Makros, a plump man of medium height, who looked somewhat lethargic, and the short, thin, fiery Dr. Spiros Fotianopoulos, who spoke fluent English. Very pleased with their find, they greeted us in joyful expectation, assured us that we would soon be well, and invited us out for dinner that same evening. Upon which we did, indeed, miraculously recover!

Towards nightfall, Dr. Lefteris Constantinides, the tall, dark, handsome doctor, took the three of us to the Reception, and the Management refused to let us pay; would not even hear of it!

"You see," said Pam, beaming like a Cheshire cat, "Greek hospitality! I knew it!"

The three cavaliers certainly seemed gallant. They drove us to a Taverna that nestled at the edge of the sea, and feasted us like deities by beach lights and starlight, to the tunes of bouzouki, while the moonlit waters lapped at our toes and enchanted us.

This was living! Pam sighed in satisfaction. Greek hospitality was indeed "as in the days of

Homer." But we had been warned: "Greeks, Yes! But Ouzo, No!" So, when the doctors took us to the dance floor and offered us drinks, we were prepared.

Romance was in the air: the dashing Dr. Lefteris Constantinides and Pamela were beaming at each other. He invited her to dance. Then in a flash, they disappeared to walk along the moonlit beach. The two left took this as the signal, and amorous advances were not long in coming, as I concentrated on drinking my Greek Mountain Shepherd's tea. The middle, plump Dr. Manolis Makros and I were obviously mismatched and the short, thin, fiery Dr. Spiros Fotianopoulos was having no luck with Maureen. So they decided to swap: I got the short, fiery, thin one, and Maureen the middle, plump one - at which point Pamela and her Adonis reappeared from their beach walk – looking somewhat subdued. But as for romance - we were a disaster! We wouldn't drink Ouzo, and we were not *properly responding*.

We had found no accommodation for that night as yet, but Dr. Manolis Makros took care of this. With great courtesy and generosity he said, "You can sleep at my house tonight."

We thanked them and said good-bye to the somewhat pale and crestfallen Drs. Constantinides and Fotianopoulos. Dr. Makros drove us to his house, showed us to our separate bedrooms, and looking somewhat depressed, he left.

Pam, Maureen and I huddled into one large bed. The night was full of strange sounds. A door creaked. Did we have a visitor that night? But three-in-the-bed must have been too much, even for the hardiest Adonis.

Next morning we tidied up, wrote a note of thanks, and left quietly without meeting our distinguished cavaliers again. Maureen returned to London.

It was at this point, and just in time for my twenty-first birthday, that Pamela, like a golden goddess, bestowed on me an unequalled boon: a five-day cruise around the Greek Islands.

Now we, too, would enter the world of the Greek *shipónas*! The sea is in the blood of the Greek! It would shortly get into ours, too!

But the islands!

We visited Crete, Rhodes, Kos, Mykonos and Delos. Unforgettable were the sunsets, the wine-red sea, and the night sky: then dawn would indeed come early, with rosy fingers, over the whitening sea.

It is impossible, here, to do the islands justice, unspoilt as they then were. I remember so clearly, even today, small incidents that touched me, such as a fleeting encounter in Patmos, when a Greek Orthodox monk passed me on the way to the monastery, and his deep, penetrating eyes met mine. It was like being pulled into a powerful magnetic force and being held within it. For a moment we stopped to stare after one another. And while sitting in a café along the harbor in Kos, having an iced coffee, I saw an olive-skinned Greek girl of around twenty-five, with a thick long black plait and deep blue eyes, maneuvering a small boat in the bay below – a goddess of striking beauty. She reminded me of Jota, the young Greek woman I had met in London.

Author (left) with her best friend, Pamela (right)

Patmos was a sheer wonder. What I loved most, was riding along the donkey trail to the Orthodox Monastery of St. John the Divine. How different it is, today, being taken up the narrow road in tourist buses that pass one another with barely an inch to spare, and then park to belch out their tourists for brief visits.

Our cruise also stopped at Halicarnassus (Bodrun) Turkey. But we hurried past the medieval castle without stopping, for we had a mission – to buy a hookah for my Uncle Joseph, a story told in *Walking Into Moments*. So we headed towards the Old Town, hoping to find one there. And we did!

The fires in Greece were finally put out. But nothing could quench the fires of memory stoked by this youthful adventure: a wild love for the incredible blue of the sea, the unique light, the whitewashed shore-lines, the sheer brilliance of the sun, moon and the stars, the fresh sea air and the Greek Islands cruise that left me with a passionate, life-long love of the islands. The sea had entered my blood.

And today, when I want to drown a sorrow or celebrate some joy, I go to the Greek tavern down the road to drink a glass of Ouzo, listen to bouzouki and dream of going back.

GETTING THROUGH CUSTOMS

MIDDLE CROSSINGS

THE LAST GOOD WOMAN

"We were both born in Israel and love it here," said Jocheved. "I just hope they'll let us live in peace."

It was 1963. One border was peaceful.

My elderly Uncle Joseph had often spoken to me about the ancient Hebrew alphabet and how each of its letters had cosmic significance. He was a man who radiated peace and wisdom. Just by tracing the Hebrew characters, he told me, one could invoke healing. He spoke passionately about Israel and the first immigrants.

"They had virtually nothing to start with," he told me. "Each family was given a tent and a goat, and all they had to eat was what they could grow. The settlers worked together and founded agricultural collectives, *Kibbutzim*, some of the earliest around 1920. What they have achieved is wonderful."

He paused a while.

"One of the touching things you will see in Jerusalem," he continued, "is the Orthodox Jews, clothed in black according to the ancient tradition, sitting outside their shops with open prayer books, uttering their prayers in the street."

He showed me a magazine article he had kept.

"Throw a stone at a *Sabra*," I read, "and he'll pick it up and start building with it."

The Sabras are the Israeli-born: proud and beautiful new nation, every young man and woman a soldier at eighteen. Many lived in the Kibbutzim, where they worked without pay in communal ownership for the common good and with participation in decision-making. The kibbutz provided for their basic needs and medical care.

Uncle's enthusiasm fired me. I wanted to discover more; to experience life in the Kibbutz for myself. I also wanted to learn this language of the sacred characters. I took long leave and set out to see for myself. I planned to stay in Israel for six months and to learn Hebrew, hopefully Ancient.

The boat from Marseilles landed at Haifa. I breathed in the unexpected heat. Before I had got half way down the gangplank, language lessons had begun.

"*Shalom*," said a young man, first thing. "Want to come to bed with me?"

"*Shalom*," I replied, taken aback. "No thank you."

"*Shalom, Shalom*!"

And off to the next one.

So this was God's land! Life was earthy,

immediate and bubbled vividly on the surface.

Language lessons were going to be secular! Over forty years have passed, but the experience is as vivid as if it had taken place yesterday.

Getting around Israel was easy in those days. People were friendly, hitchhiking was safe, and one could reduce costs by working one's way round the *Kibbutzim*.

Visitors only had to work half-day. In exchange they were given food and lodging, a blue or beige cloth hat, toothpaste, soap and some stamps. In London, I had met a young man who had just returned from six months in Israel. He gave me the address of a Kibbutz south of Haifa.

"Find Dov and Hannah. Tell them I sent you."

They were easy to find; everyone knew them.

"A friend of Michael's is a friend of ours," said Hannah, making me welcome. "You can choose where you want to work; indoors or out."

Lodged in a small wooden hut with a Turkish girl, I joined the apple-pickers. The alarm rang at four-thirty in the morning while it was still cool (the maximum average temperature would be rising to 30.8 degrees) and in the communal dining-room were laid out rations of bread and butter, jam and tea, just to start us off. At five a.m. a trailer pulling tractor, driven by a field superintendent, drove the volunteers to the apple orchards. The trailer was laden with ladders, large bushels and smaller baskets, and we all rattled along in it. When we reached our field, the ladders were propped up against the trees, and we strapped the baskets to our waist, and climbed the ladder. I loved this. Before the morning was properly under way, three hours' work up a ladder was done, with one's head in colorful, sweet-smelling, heavy-laden branches.

The tractor came for us at eight and drove us back again for breakfast. Kibbutzniks worked hard and long by personal commitment, and came back ravenous. Breakfast seemed like a celebration: bread and jam, eggs, yoghurt, curd cheese, freshly picked cucumbers, large sweet onions, green peppers, tomatoes, and the sweetest midget bananas straight from the plantation, as well as milk, tea and coffee. After breakfast we were driven back to the fields for the second shift, and for us visitors, the day's work ended at noon.

Meals at the Kibbutz were served in the communal dining-room at long tables and benches parallel to one another, and the noise was deafening. It only quieted a little when the workers set to with gusto. Food was available in unlimited quantities; except for meat, which was served in portions. And the taste of the home-grown vegetables was wonderful. Suppers were light, and similar to breakfast: Salami, avocadoes and olives were added to the morning's fare.

Dov and Hannah were around forty, and obviously very much in love. In fact, I thought they had just got married. Friendly, open, and tremendously welcoming, they told me part of their story. They had joined the Kibbutz at the beginning, when everyone lived in tents. "All we had to eat was the tomatoes we grew. We even made tomato jam. But to this day our children can't stand the sight of a tomato!"

By 1960 the first signs of wealth had appeared in the Kibbutz. The progress from tents to wooden huts led to the building of very small apartments for those who had been there longest. Dov and Hannah lived in one of these. Their hospitality was wonderful.

"They're obviously on honeymoon!" I said to a neighbor.

"Dov and Hannah?" The woman burst out laughing. "They married very young and quarreled violently for about twenty years. Once we even thought they were going to kill each other. Then one day, they fell head over heels in love! And that's the way it has been ever since."

"This afternoon our daughter will come to visit," said Hannah. (Children were raised communally and separately, and the older children had assigned duties in the kibbutz.)

"But this is beginning to change," she continued, "for it has not turned out very satisfactory."

(Since 1997 no Kibbutz has separate

children's quarters any more, and families may now have dinner at home and spend the evening privately instead of communally, if they so wish.)

I hoped to attend the daily Hebrew class in the afternoons, but language training was only made available to immigrants who were to be at the Kibbutz for a full year. So I was not admitted.

However, with or without Hebrew, one was soon drawn into frequent interchange.

There was amazing vitality in this land; the very earth vibrated through one. Nowhere else did my hair ever shine as it did in Israel.

One way or another, this energy surged and made itself felt. Invitations were offered with startling simplicity. Best to learn the language for this at once!

There were four greetings one absolutely had to know:

Boker tov - Good morning
Erev tov - Good evening
Laila tov - Good night.

And of course, *Shalom* - frequently followed by - "Which do you prefer: *Good evening* or *Good night?*"

In those days, in the Israel of the 1960s; one did not need much vocabulary. Everyone was a *comrade;* to designate any other person, just use the word *haver.* Nor did one need to know how to count to more than three.

Ehhad - one
Shtayim - two: *us-two*
Shalosh - three: when two are not alone!

Communication was simple and direct. It always began with the greeting *Shalom!* This would soon be followed by *us-two-comrades*, with an offer to *laila tov*, to-go-good-night.

And then there was that vital word *LO*, which quite definitely meant *NO!*

With plenty of eyebrows, gestures and smiles, I soon became an expert in this new language. But I remained relatively detached.

"I already have *ehhad haver* - in London!" I would insist. "One comrade back there, to whom I'm faithful!"

"Oh well, Shalom!"

And that's where it would end. This open approach seemed so natural.

I was fascinated by the sheer feline beauty of the young; they belonged to a new, uninhibited race, proud of their land and their freedom. I would watch the military vehicles as they drove by. It always surprised me to see how beautiful were the young soldier-girls, sitting beside each other, holding their guns.

The work and commitment to the communal good on the Kibbutz was intense. Because of the burning heat, everyone had a long break after lunch, and only resumed work around three. But when Jeff, a young American arrived, he did not do likewise. Instead of taking a siesta, he went back to the fields right after lunch and continued to work until supper. The Israelis said they had never ever seen anyone work like him.

It was a strict Kibbutz rule that the *Rosh Hashanah* celebrations were private; and that no outsiders were to be invited. But Hannah and Dov took me with them anyway. I did not understand the words, but could feel the beauty and power and hope as the young sang and all those present joined in prayer.

One month later I moved on. With my shoulder bag and blue cloth hat, vital in the burning sun, I hitchhiked up the road till darkness fell. Then I simply made for the nearest Kibbutz, where I was shown to a wooden hut, usually shared by three young men currently away on military duty. Next morning I was given work: picking grapes with a group of adolescent immigrants in rehabilitation. I loved being among the vines; Eve could not have asked for more.

A few days later, I was introduced to a plump, dark-haired woman who spoke English. She was visiting her cousin, who lived in this Kibbutz. She stared at me intently for a while, then fired a volley of questions at me:

What was I doing in Israel?

And how did I get to this Kibbutz anyway?

Did I have any children? And *why* not?

Was I married? And why *not*?

Did I *at least* have a boyfriend?

I met this onslaught meekly, and when through, she said, "I'm Jocheved. When you are near Tel Aviv, phone me, and come to stay."

Two weeks later, ten miles from Tel Aviv, I phoned to ask whether she still meant it.

"Lunch is hot, your room is ready," she said. "Why did it take you so long?"

When I arrived, Jocheved embraced me as if she had known me all my life. Then she introduced me to her husband, who emerged in a wheelchair. She had a three-year-old son, whom she adored. She was teaching him to whistle and was enormously proud of his little-bird attempts to copy her.

"You can have Joshua's room," she said, and promptly moved him out.

The family lived in a pleasant, cool house with an open inner courtyard. David had lost both of his legs in the World War II. At that time Jocheved had been a field nurse. Her eyes sparkled as she remembered.

"I fell in love with his blue eyes, the moment I saw him lying injured in the tent. Later he got new legs. Today he can do everything. Even play tennis!"

Jocheved treated me like a member of the family. She cooked Middle Eastern meals, with delicious fresh vegetables. I loved being with them. Every morning she mopped the stone floors of every room as well as the inner courtyard. Their home was sparklingly clean.

"And they say that Jews are dirty!" she said scornfully.

"You are welcome to stay as long as you like," she continued, as I helped her clean. I stayed for a week. Her husband even found the time to drive me around Tel Aviv.

From there I took a coach trip to Eilat, and saw how the Israelis had made the desert bloom. The bus bumped along over the red majestic desert track in the sweltering heat, until quite suddenly everything was green! Here one could buy sweet, cool grapes, straight from the desert vineyards.

Now I learned the right word for this: *Yoffie!*

It meant wonderful, most wonderful. And absolutely whooping.

Yoffie! said the folks who saw the cool green grapes.

Yoffie! I echoed, sinking my teeth into their flesh.

Yoffie! had said the young fellow back there at the gangplank as he spied me, ripe for the picking. Hebrew classes were live, and definitely modern. With *Shalom, haver, boker tov, erev tov* and *laila tov and yoffie* - my vocabulary was complete.

That, and a good thumb for hitchhiking, was all one needed.

Next I found my way to a much smaller Kibbutz, under the Golan Heights on the north-east borders of Israel and Syria, where I joined the grape-pickers.

One of the elders told me a story.

"It is hard to find privacy on a Kibbutz," he began. "Well, not long ago on this kibbutz, there was a young couple, desperately in love. Now, this farm has only one tractor. One Sunday afternoon, the two of them decided to borrow the tractor to steal away for some private moments. They had barely come to a halt in the fields, when shots suddenly rained down on them from the Golan Heights, the rocky plateau some 6,500 feet above them. (Captured by Israel in 1967 and annexed in 1981). Alarmed, they hid under the tractor until the shooting stopped. There they remained till darkness fell, then drove back to their kibbutz unharmed. But they looked very sheepish when they were asked to explain why the tractor was limping!"

I stayed in this community for a week. Many older Europeans lived there, too, and talking with them was easy. They were quieter and very different from the Sabras in their ways - more cultured and courteous. More poetical. One older gentleman, who took to me, even became quite lyrical.

I arrived in Jerusalem late one afternoon. Feeling rather lost in the hustle and bustle of the central station, I looked around for some help. I knew that many of the taxi drivers were also tourist guides, well-known for their culture and ability to speak many languages. So I decided to treat myself to a single taxi ride through the centre of Jerusalem to my hostel. I found a driver who spoke English, and got in. He was an older man with a pleasant voice. Before depositing me at the convent near the City Gate, he said, "Would you like to come on tour with me? I'll show you all around for free." Surprised and delighted, I accepted his offer.

Bullet marks pocked the walls of the convent and a guard stood on the roof. There was an inexpensive basement dormitory, empty save for a girl from Eastern Europe, and a lot of mice. Sporadic shots could be heard at night. Jerusalem was being shot into. But no one shot back.

The tourist guide turned up two days later as promised. He seemed very pleased with himself.

"Now there are only the two of us," he said with that look in his eye.

"Are you married?" I asked hesitantly, once we were on our way.

"Sure!" he said. "I even have three children. But I have time in the afternoon."

"But I don't go out with married men!"

"You *don't?* But *all* the women come here for that!"

"They *do?*"

"Yes. They come from the Scandinavia countries and many other places. They complain that their husbands are cold or something."

"Really?"

"You mean you didn't know?"

I kept quiet.

Evidently, both the men and the women here

were perfectly forthright!

"You're different," he said suddenly, in an odd kind of way. "That's OK! I'll take you on a tour all the same. Just for the fun of it, nothing more."

The following morning he picked me up, and set out on a long drive to the Judean hills. On the way he pointed out a few sacred sites - somewhat distractedly - I thought. All at once his face lit up.

"I know what's wrong with you!" he declared. "You're a virgin!"

I grinned. So, he'd been mulling things over! After a long silence, "Well then, you must be a blue stocking!"

I chuckled: a cold intellectual indeed!

Up in the Judean hills my guide parked the car to let me enjoy the view of Jerusalem below. He got out and came to stand beside me. I thought he would point out the landmarks and relate their history. But he was much too preoccupied. His brow furrowed, till he suddenly burst out with, "Now I've got it! You're one of those women who only like women." My laughter shook him.

Then, to my unutterable amazement, the man turned lyrical.

"You are *Yoffie! Yoffie! Yoffie!*" he chanted. "Indeed, you are the *last* good woman!"

Whereupon he drove me back to the hostel and dropped me off with perfect decorum.

I loved being in Israel, and in between working on the kibbutzim, I made my pilgrimage to the Christian sacred sites: Galilee, Jerusalem, Nazareth, and Bethlehem, only eight kilometers away. There were moments that touched me deeply: a walk through Jerusalem's old city, the men praying at the Wailing Wall; the startling proximity of the three faiths - Jewish, Christian and Muslim - with their 300 places of worship: synagogues, churches, mosques and monuments. And in particular, Bethlehem, where I met an old Arab man sitting and eating on the steps of his house in a narrow cobbled street. He smiled at me so warmheartedly, broke his bread and gave me half.

Time passed so quickly; it had become mid-October. But the burning heat was exhausting. Reluctantly I decided to leave after only two and a half months. I had not learned ancient Hebrew, but had seen wonders: though the last was still to come.

My ticket eluded me. I went to collect it in Tel Aviv, only to be told it had been sent to Haifa.

I hitchhiked up the coast to fetch it in Haifa, but it had been sent back to Tel Aviv.

Back in Tel Aviv, they said,

"So sorry, there must be some mistake; the ticket's been sent back to Haifa."

Hitchhiking was usually safe and easy in Israel. Drivers were generous and quick to stop. I had taken rides in all sorts of cars, among them a black sedan with an elegant Arab gentleman, and a battered blue truck full of squawking chickens, driven by a Romanian. The day before my charter flight was due to leave, I finally found my ticket in Tel Aviv, and early in the morning, stood on the side of the road once more, thumb out, waiting.

But no car passed. Not even one. Not that particular morning!

The road was swelteringly hot; as the hours passed, the temperature kept rising. I was on my final lap to visit a family to whom my Uncle had given me a letter of introduction. It was midday when a car finally appeared.

"Netanya?"

"OK! Netanya!" (Centre district of Israel)

I got in gratefully, confident that my by now extended vocabulary had equipped me for virtually everything.

"Shalom," I greeted him, as he drove on. "Do you speak *English - French - German?"*

"No!"he boomed, *"Tourk!"*

I knew nothing of the splendors of the Ottoman Empire, but there flashed into my mind a line from a poem I learned at school about the Turks at the time of the Crusades:

"and with his scimitar split them clean in two."

"I want to get out," I gestured. "Right here!"

Unperturbed, *this* Turk smiled at me reassuringly and said, *"You* tourist, *I* tourist! I am not going to knife you!"

With a sleight of the hand he made as if to

draw a keen blade out of his right knee-length sock, brandished it in the air, shook his head vigorously, and with a hearty laugh, tucked the imaginary knife back into the sock.

"Anyway why stop at Netanya?" he continued with perfect composure. "*We-two* could drive up North, all *romantique,* and I could show you around this place and that. Then we could picnic under a tree, and go-good-night-ing under the stars!"

His eyes lit up at the thought of such unlimited promise.

"*Lo!*" I said. "Most certainly not! I have one comrade in London. *Ehhad haver!*"

"Are you *sure*? London is far away, you know! Much too far for him to find out!"

The mere thought made his eyes sparkle.

But I pointed to my heart and repeated firmly: "One comrade in London."

"*Aha!*" he said, a fountain of smiles. "You are a good woman, I see! So you can belong to your *one comrade* down to your middle." His hand sliced the air clean in two. Then, overcome by the sheer weight of genius, he added, "Down to your waist for *your* man - and all the rest for *me*!"

Unable to contain my surprise, I replied, "Oh! Thank you, thank you! But my friend in London would be most upset."

This had no effect on him whatsoever; neither did the tears I traced down my cheeks. So I shook my head gravely and said: "Allah would not like this. He really would not!"

Now this required his full attention. The man drew up the car at the side of the road and turned to face me earnestly. Then he placed his right index and middle finger lightly on his thumb, relaxed his wrist in the typical gesture, and raised his hand above my head.

Yoffie! he burst out, *Yoffie!*

His hand made little circles in the air, going down past my chin, my neck, my chest and from stop to stop, his voice rose in crescendo, *Yoffie! Yoffie! Yoffie!*

He sighed passionately, and his hand continued to circle to the beat of this mantra, till it reached my feet. Whereupon he threw back his head, closed his eyes fervently, sighed deeply, opened them once more, and pointing to the Heavens declared:

Allah would approve of you,
Oh *Allah* would
And so do I,
For the top and the bottom half of you are
Absolutely Y O F F I E !

And with this blessing, he dropped me off courteously at Netanya where I knocked at Naomi's door. She was a young woman to whom Uncle had given me a letter of introduction. Within minutes I was spilling out my latest adventure. Much to her delight. Then she swapped a story.

"I used to live in Cairo," she told me, "and my parents were determined to marry me off. So my mother would invite eligible men, that is, those whom *she* considered eligible. So every afternoon I had to sit there politely at tea-time, while she introduced me to yet another man. But you should have *seen* the men she brought! They were middle-aged, balding and fat; one uglier than the other. I refused every single one of them. And yet, my mother kept bringing me more. In the end I ran away to London. There I fell in love with an Englishman and got married. Now we live here and are very happy."

We sat outside on the terrace of their lovely home, enjoying the fresh air, while she served tea with home-made Egyptian pastries and my favorite *Rahat Lokoum* (Turkish Delight, at one time also known in England as "lumps of delight!") that I had first tasted in Cairo.

"The autumn weather here is wonderful," Naomi told me. "One can always eat outside and be sure it will not rain. My husband and I really love living in Israel."

In 1993 (no longer of vine-leaf age) I returned to Jerusalem to do a course on "Instrumental Enrichment," designed by Professor Reuven Feuerstein, a world-renowned cognitive psychologist, to help underachievers reach their potential.

It was then that I discovered that the immigrant youths with whom as a young woman I had picked grapes in the Kibbutz, had been his protégés.

Finally I managed to locate Talma, the wonderful Instrumental Enrichment teacher, and sent her this story.

I shall always cherish her reply.

> Yes, this was Israel.
> Your nice story is now a piece of history that you described so beautifully. In a short story you gave a panoramic view of our little state as it was. While reading it I had a feeling of going back in a time tunnel. It was like a dream.

As I watch the news today, my heart goes out to all those who live in the Middle East, on both sides of the borders, as they endeavor to work towards peace.

THE RISING SCREAM

When Uncle Joseph died, and my father passed away twenty-four hours later, I developed trouble with the *rising scream*. It sat in my guts, ready to bolt up my chest and rocket out of my throat. It lurked, like a monster in the deep, between me and what I *should* be.

The rising scream is a secret terror, sequestered n the depths of one's belly. I used to be terrified that if ever it escaped - that scream - it would be heard all the way to Cape Town. I thought that once let loose, it would sear across continents. I lived with the threat of the rising scream and felt it run up and down my sinews, menacingly. It inhabited me for a long, long while. My throat began to tighten!

The rising scream smolders like a volcano in one's subterranean self, ready to burst and climb steeply up the scale. One dare not tell anyone, not even oneself: *nice girls* don't scream! It has a will of its own, and when something will no longer let itself be bottled up, it simply breaks out.

One should never, never scream; a nice girl does not.

It was in London, that I first observed the rising scream at work. Our landlady, Lady Horace, the owner of a magnificent three-storey mansion, was in the habit of harassing us when she was in residence. We had to walk through the front hall and first floor of her house to get to our top-floor furnished apartment, and so it was easy for her to nab us. After all, the whole great mansion was hers. It was situated near Hampstead Heath, opposite the old church steeple, in Cannon Place, so named because the pavements were lined with cannons from the Battle of Waterloo - and still are. It was her top floor *nursery* that she let to us three girls - two South Africans (from *the Colonies*), friends from schooldays, and a pleasant blond American schoolteacher, who from time to time let out blood-curdling screams at night, for which she took pills.

For servants Lady Horace kept two fair-skinned, unmarried sisters, only somewhat younger than she; in fact, she had *owned* them since they were eighteen. They had sweet, gentle faces, and were always neatly dressed in a white apron and cap. They lit the coal fires each morning, cleaned the house, cooked, washed and ironed; and in all things they obeyed their employer with deference and respect. She lodged them in the cold, dark, damp basement of her house. They served her faithfully until they became old and frail. Then she considered them of no further use.

Lady Horace did not favor our talking to her servants. But one Sunday, when she was away, we went down to the cold, damp basement and knocked at their door. They invited us in to their sparsely furnished room, and made us very welcome. They were happy to have a chat.

"We got our board and lodgings, but very little pay," the younger of the two sisters told us.

"'Twas only pocket-money," said the older lady, coughing as she drew her knitted shawl closer over her shoulders. "And now we are *a bit too poorly* with arthritis to be able to go on working."

"So, you see," continued the younger, "we were not able to save a thing for our retirement. And we haven't any pension. So we've decided to move up North to live with a cousin who offered to take us in." She spoke with the sweet, innocent smile of one who has made peace with her life. These two dear people - true ladies if ever there some - had graced the house for fifty years.

"We are going to miss you both," I said.

We, the lodgers, were expected to lead our daily lives as if we did not live there at all. Our main function, we were to discover, was to keep *the nursery* clean. But apparently we were not as good at it as her aged servants.

One day Lady Horace came up unexpectedly when I was alone. She cast a disdainful glance at the furniture and raised her eyebrows.

"Isn't this place a trifle dusty?" she said,

running her white-gloved hand over the surface of the teak desk. "The banisters could do with a polish, too!"

Discomfort inhabited us and settled into our bones.

My friend was in the habit of conducting herself as a lady – which, in certain circumstances, meant bottling it. But one day, while washing dishes in the kitchen of our top-floor flat, let to us by this genuine English lady, right there in Cannon Place, with the whole English history of the Battle of Waterloo behind it, all the way back to 1812 – she picked up a wine glass, and with a quick, sharp flick of her hand, pitched it out of the window.

Then she stood there stiffly, watching as the glass plummeted down like a tipsy helicopter, and exploded on the cemented back yard outside Lady Horace's living room.

Whereupon she drew herself up to her full stature, donned her best *English Voice* (her accent being that of a South African from Cape Town), and marched off to find the startled landlady standing at her drawing-room window, utterly amazed.

"Oh, Lady Horace, I am s-o-o-o- sorry," she said, in her most lady-like tones. "I was washing up and the glass just happened to fall out of the window. I'll replace it, of course. May I walk through your lounge to pick up the pieces?"

Thereupon she went to collect the shrill, sharp, shattered fragments of her withheld scream, and placed them neatly in a bag for disposal!

One should never, never scream; a nice girl does not.

But sometime later I discovered that a scream can carry one from one place to another.

We heard that Lady Horace was going to go to Australia for three months, and that she would be letting her living quarters, and we were delighted. Thus it was that a *man* moved into the rooms beneath.

We were curious about him, and invited him up for a drink. We had never had *a man* up in our apartment before. He told us stories and we refilled his glass. In fact, he turned out to be Lady Horace's nephew. He had square shoulders and brown hair, and looked solid and reliable. Otherwise he was in no way remarkable.

He related how his wife, an Australian, had wanted to go back out there for good, and how he had agreed to pack up and leave England. She had gone on ahead while he stayed behind to sell the house and wind up their affairs. Having done most of that, he moved temporarily into the rooms below.

"My wife gave me ten years here in England. Now she wants to go back to Australia. I feel I have had my share. I have already sold the house, and so my Aunt let me live here till I had completed my preparations."

Nephew or not, we thought it amazing that Lady Horace had actually permitted a man to cross her threshold, let alone live in her house! Now her absence freed us to step into the sacred precincts!

"I know it must seem extravagant," he went on to tell us, "and that to others it makes no sense, but my wife is getting *her* Australia, and I want to take *my* car. With me going out there, I must have my *very own* car, and not any other."

As we filled his glass once more, he confided, "I knew it was time to give my wife her chance, because she had started to scream - something she had never done before. And when a woman screams you never forget it!"

Later we two, the South African girls, found a good reason to go down to help him with his packing! He thanked us, but thought he could manage on his own. We traipsed back up the stairs again. But still curious about this man, I found another excuse to go back a bit later, this time alone. He pointed at the large boxes on the armchair, waiting to be stuffed into his already overfull suitcase lying on the bed.

"I don't know how I am ever going to fit them in; they are presents for my children. I have three boys."

Suddenly his eyes lit up. "That was rather naughty of you girls yesterday. You made me slightly tipsy."

Then his eyes clouded over. The man

fidgeted with the straps of his suitcase. Then he looked at me, the suitcase and the bed, and once more at me - somewhat strangely - I thought, and said, "I could do you a power of no good. But I won't. You see, I promised to be true. And I am."

We had become very fond of the Englishman who had lodged, for only a week, in our landlady's mansion, and were sorry the day he left for the ship that was to take him and his car to Melbourne. The house felt empty without him, and as we passed his room on our way out, we noticed he had left the door slightly ajar. As we pushed it open to peep in, a ragged scrap of paper fluttered onto the floor. We picked it up and pored over it: "Borrow £5,000.-" it read.

So that's what it had taken to get him to Australia!

That was the only sign someone had been there! We were sad to see him go, but his visit had made us feel so much more at home than before.

Then, with the end of the school term, our American flat-sharer left to return home.

One should never, never scream; a nice girl does not.

The next time I observed the lurking menace in action, was when it hit a friend of ours who lived in Geneva. And it was she who would much later tell the story.

Forty-year-old Delia had the presence of a model. She was perfect, not only in her daily living, but also as a hostess. She had been perfect for over twelve years. If she ever had a problem, she never showed it.

Her hearty, popular American husband worked from home, and loved to surround himself with people. People came to consult him every day, sometimes in groups, sometimes on their own. From time to time one or other of them simply decided to move in. Delia took it all in her stride, gracefully. She never murmured, never complained, and in her frequent appearances with her husband in public, she remained calm, serene and positive, not a single hair out of place.

Finally the day came when her husband decided to return to America. Delia and the children were delighted. Preparations began at once. The house turned into a kind of crazy shambles. When they had finally packed all that they wanted to take with them, huge piles of things were left over for the garage sale: everything imaginable from theatre costumes to walls full of books, Christmas decorations, old hats and lots of plain junk.

I was amazed at the incredible quantity of oddments for sale.

"How on earth did you manage to accumulate so much stuff??" I asked. Delia screwed up her face and replied acidly, "What none of you realize is that I have never, *ever,* been free to live in this house alone! Most of this stuff is not even mine. Lots of people come to stay, then simply leave their junk behind. But I'm going to make sure that this never happens to me again."

Then one day bottling it up no longer worked. Suddenly one night, at dinner with the family, and without warning, Delia's mouth opened. A scream arose as if from the soles of her feet. It pitched itself forward and filled the room. A stunned moment; frozen shock. Her seventeen-year-old son rushed to the windows and closed them. The scream continued. Her husband stared at her in disbelief, but the scream continued to pierce the air. Her teenage daughter got up and went to put her arms around her mother. The husband began to look uncomfortable and hung his head.

Then, without any reference to her will, and in its own time, her scream died down.

"No one more surprised than I," Delia confided later. "I couldn't have stopped screaming if I had wanted to!"

Her husband made a concession: from then on he would have people come to the house only six days a week - not seven!

The rising scream respects no boundaries: neither time nor space; nor age, nor country.

Thirty years later my London friend of the shattered glass, now living in Western Australia, found it lurking within her once more.

This time, it wasn't a problem with royalty, but with the neighbors. They argued all the time, at full blast. They bellowed at their children and the children bellowed back. The most intimate details of their life became public. Their radios and television blared - seven days a week. They broadcast their lives as through a megaphone. In her own home, my friend found she could no longer have a simple conversation with her husband, and be heard. For a long time her muscles tightened to hold in the invisible rage, and she did nothing to let it out. She had been brought up to be a *nice girl,* and such she would remain.

Then she understood for the first time that no amount of polite negotiation was going to get her anywhere. And still she held it in. Till the day came when the sheer unfairness of it all fuelled her into action. Her jaw firmly set, she took her clean, empty, galvanized iron dustbin and a big, metal spoon, and went to stand right beside the neighbor's wall. There she turned the dustbin upside down, and began to drum on it with all her might. She banged on it till she had banged out all her pent-up rage and she could bang no more.

Many years later she wrote: "Three-quarters of the fun of making a din, called music for an excuse, is to force other people to endure it! But the other quarter is the enjoyment of the rhythm. What the banging on the dustbin did was to set up an irresistible counter rhythm - a good African one:

BANG bang, bang, bang, BANG bang bang,
Ka bang, Ka bang, BANG BANG.

"Do this fifty times, and noisemakers can't stand it! That big spoon split right down the middle."

The neighbors could not withstand her rising scream.

They had built their house, argued and bellowed in it. Six weeks later they moved out.

Her story made me feel much better.

HIGHLY UNUSUAL

On February 27th 2008, World Travel Watch sent this alert for Barbados:

> Crime against tourists is low here and usually takes the form of petty theft, but twice in January tourist groups on guided tours of the island were held up at gunpoint. In the second incident shots were fired but no one was hurt. Police believe they have identified some of the perpetrators, and the U.S. Embassy in Bridgetown reported the incidents as "highly unusual."

"Highly Unusual" is a euphemism that veils the myths and mysteries of Caribbean innuendo. In 1974 in Trinidad, at the Piarco airport in Port-of-Spain, it meant I was being taken for a spy.

I was to be the guest of Uncle Joe, an eighty-year old pastor I had met in Hampstead, North London. He wanted to set up a holiday package for the English elderly to go to Trinidad, and I had long dreamt of living on an island. We liked each other enormously and so he simply invited me. "I will have a house and a car for you," he said. The opportunity had looked ideal.

"What are you doing here?" asked the Immigration Officer, eyeing my two young sons skeptically. I tried to tell him. "This is highly unusual!" he grunted. "And how do you expect to live?"

"I went to see the High Commissioner in London. He told me that with my qualifications, it would be quite easy for me to find a job in Trinidad."

"Oh, those people don't know anything!" he snapped. "You'll have to take the next plane back."

I had burnt my bridges; had come over 7,000 kilometers, for this? But if not back, then where to?

At last Uncle Joe arrived to fetch me at the airport. Tall, straight, well - spoken, courteous but very firm, he pleaded for me. The official shook his head, repeated his threat, and gave me twenty-four hours to leave. Uncle Joe drove me to his home, deposited me at his neighbors, (the house he promised me was still being built) and went to consult his bishop. The Bishop obtained a reprieve. But Immigration had a suspect's file – one that was to decide my fate. It was a file on a man whose surname was almost the same as mine. Just one letter was different. The situation did not look good. On the second day the water was cut and this was followed by a postal strike. Immigration gave me two weeks to get out; it was final. By then I had no regrets. Uncle Joe took me to the small wooden Mount Horeb Pentecostal church and together with six old men, he prayed for us.

"The Lord will protect you," he said, laying his hands on my head. "Go to Barbados. The pastor there is my friend. He will welcome you."

And that is I found myself en route for the neighboring island, my final destination. Barbados is some 200 kilometers away.

Pastor Vaughn, a man with a deeply kind face, fetched us at Christchurch airport, and drove us to St. James in his old grey van, up a dirt road called The Gap, into the Garden, to his house beside his church.

The CEF Miracle Centre, St. James, Barbados

From then on I became part of a Christian community in which every other person is called a *sister or brother*.

The CEF Miracle Centre is part of the Caribbean Evangelical Fellowship and still stands today, not far from the sea. It was built by the pastor himself, a carpenter who had faith in the Word of the Lord.

"The Holy Spirit was the architect," he told me one day with a smile. "I had been fasting and praying for guidance. On the sixth day the Holy Spirit got me out of bed at four in the morning and down on my knees, told me to take paper and a pencil and to start drawing. In a few minutes I had the entire plan of the church. I only had forty dollars, but with that I bought planks, and set to work."

The Miracle Centre was the thriving centre of the community. Prayer, education, music and celebration all took place within it. It held promise and talent. Services were accompanied by a wonderful community band.

"You know, Sis," the pastor told me one day, "the musicians had no training. They have just grown up in the church. They were not so good in the beginning, but the Holy Spirit took them in hand."

I thought the early Christians must have been like this.

Pastor Vaughn labored tirelessly to upgrade the premises, and to educate his community, and soon a meeting room with modern conveniences was added. In the day-time he held an outside job. Back in his little office at the end of the day, he worked on church matters until late at night. Many times he was called out to minister elsewhere, to visit the sick or to cast out evil spirits.

One day one of the church brothers told me: "Before we got electricity all over Barbados, there used to be a lot of bad spirits lurking around in the dark lanes. Some of them were just a plain nuisance. Sometimes I would come home and find my things scattered around the house. At others, there would be something pulling the blankets off me at night. But most of the streets are lit now, so we have less of this. They don't like the light."

When they became sick, the members of this community did not go to the doctor, but would, with quiet confidence, pray their way through. "That is our way," the pastor told me. So when I went down with a very painful ear infection, I thought I would try it. But Pastor Vaughn took me to the doctor himself. "This is not for you," he insisted. "We are used to it; you are not."

Pas Vaughn treated me with unfailing old world courtesy and extended many acts of kindness, as did his very practical wife. Their help was vital in getting through many first-time situations.

Everything was accomplished through

prayer and faith. One day a young woman told me how she met her husband. "I had never even spoken to him," she said. "But when I wanted to get married, I just went to church and told the Lord. That is what we all did. One day he put a picture of my future husband into my heart. At the same time he placed a picture of me in his. That is how we knew we were meant for each other. But until then I had just waited and prayed. And today we are married."

I witnessed a tremendous, continuing surge for self-improvement, but the gap between those who lived in wooden houses, and those who lived in "wall houses" seemed almost unbridgeable.

I met several American mothers whose husbands were on a three year stint to improve their careers through hands-on experience. By comparison, the houses they had rented looked like royal mansions. Sometimes I would be asked to babysit while one of them returned home for a brief visit. So I tasted the difference.

I made many friends among both the White and the Black population while I was in Barbados. There were many invitations, much sharing. But what I remember most clearly, was the early advice of one caring brother: "If ever you don't have enough to eat, just go visiting. People will cut whatever they have in half and share it with you."

It took time to find a job, so I began to give pre-yoga classes, which were of interest in the

White community. Later a vacancy for an English teacher arose in a convent school.

That year I remained as much as possible within the community, and lived a simple life among them. I felt at home in my little wooden house, with its outside toilet in which frogs croaked at night. There I felt I was with my own people. I did not feel the need to frequent tourist spots or the beaches reserved for members of a club, and thus I experienced a very different side of life in Barbados.

The children did enormously enjoy the local beach.

My oldest son, imitating the local boys

The young lads on the beach had lithe, graceful bodies. I was in great admiration of their beauty.

But one day one of them decided it could be great fun to tease the "white lady" and chased me with a live octopus! And how I ran!

Even in those benign days, Pastor Vaughn spoke with warm regret about the days gone by.

"Barbados used to be a real paradise, you know, Sis. When I was little, we had plenty of avocados. One could just go and pick them. Today it is so expensive to buy one. Mothers would give their children a tablespoon of castor oil once a week, and there was plenty of fresh fruit. So we had little illness. Our people worked on the sugar cane plantations and were always busy." He sighed, a deep, deep sigh. "But in time they got lazy, and began to complain that the work was too hard for them. Soon they imported people from St. Lucia to labor in their place. Now they complain that they can't find work. And criminality has begun to creep in."

Church services were the high points of the week. Whenever he preached, the gentle pastor would suddenly turn into a lion; a lion of God.

He would begin quietly, eloquently, reading a text from the scriptures, and speak what was in his heart that day, while, with mounting fervor, the congregation would respond loudly: *Alleluia! Yes, Lord! Oh Father! Praise the Lord!*

Then the Holy Spirit would overtake him, surging up within him and pounding every muscle of his body into fiery and eloquent expression. Inspired thus, he could see into the future and prophesy.

The members of the congregation were likewise moved: some began to talk in tongues, while others translated. One unforgettable Sunday the pastor described, in detail, the violence that would erupt and escalate in the Middle East. When I read the news in Geneva, many years later, it was virtually word for word what Pastor Vaughn had predicted, so far away, so long ago. I could clearly see again the man, humble and self-effacing in daily life, who in that sermon, had turned into the Lion of God.

Some weeks after I had arrived, I went over to the pastor's house, and found him on the phone. When he put the receiver down, he said, "Yesterday the Holy Spirit told me to have a Revival. A brother from central Barbados has just called, telling me that the Holy Spirit had given him the same message. We shall have church every day for fourteen days. There will be prayer and fasting, day and night."

Pastor Vaughn kept prayer vigil at all hours; at night a few members dropped in by and by. The pastor's house was next to the church, and mine beside his. The children were quite safe, so I joined them.

On the first day of the Revival, the pastor had announced: "On the seventh day there will be a Holy Ghost healing service. The sick will be able to bring their needs to the altar."

What could I ask for? I was not ill. It came to me in the days of prayer that followed. I had inherited oversensitive ears. But decades of inner ear infections from childhood on, and a huge boil in my right ear that had hospitalized me as an adult, had made this much worse. Loud sound was torture; the louder the sound, the sharper the pain. And in this church I found myself immersed in hours of passionate preaching, music and praise. I often felt completely overwhelmed by the sheer volume of it, and would sit at the very back of the church, as far from the band as I could. Certain sounds would hit my ears like knives and shoot through my whole body. It had never occurred to me that this could ever change.

On the seventh day, a Sunday, Pastor Vaughn exhorted his congregation to have faith. He prayed with great intensity and enjoined the people to do likewise. The band played with gusto; trumpets blew, cymbals clashed, and the Assembly sang with all their might. The energy rose to bursting point. Pastor Vaughn began to speak in tongues.

When the moment was right, he gave the Altar Call. One by one, with bowed heads, those with a need filed up. Humbly they knelt at the altar. The assistant joined Pastor Vaughn in fervent prayer as, laying their hands on the sick, they called on the Holy Spirit to bless and heal.

And still I held back, sound cutting into my ears. Till at last, I, too, went to kneel at the altar. Pastor Vaughn leaned down to me and very quietly asked, "What is your need, Sister?"

"My ears hurt most of the time. Badly."

Both pastors laid their hands over my ears and began to pray aloud. As their intercession rose into the Heavens, their hands swelled. Their bodies became as lightening conductors and poured power into my ears. I sank into a swirling ocean, lost in the cresting waves.

Pastor Vaughn said, "Go in peace."

Suddenly sleepy, I went back to my seat.

When everyone had returned to their seats, the band broke into joyful celebration and the congregation burst into triumphant praise.

Alleluia! Yes Lord!
Thank you, Lord!
Praise God.

The next day the Holy Ghost healing service was followed by the feet washing ceremony. Our pastor obeyed Christ's injunction to the letter:

"… If I then, your Lord and Master, have washed your feet; ye also ought to wash one another's feet. For I have given you an example that ye should do as I have done to you…"

Thus, that day in the Miracle Centre, we washed the feet of the person sitting next to us. An old lady washed mine, and I hers.

After my return to Europe, I kept in touch with the pastor and his wife. I wanted to express my boundless gratitude for what they had done for me. In time I founded a new home, and began sorting out our surplus items to send. Among these was a small, flat portable typewriter that ran on ribbons, and was to become the pastor's main office tool for the next decade, and a pair of binoculars, that to my greatest joy, was to become a source of delight for Pastor Vaughn's few spare moments.

"You know, Sis," he wrote, "I love to watch the stars. Late at night I go outside spying in the beautiful Heavens. Oh, God's wonderful, wonderful world! Praise the Lord."

One day I packed some clothes into the only box at hand; a somewhat flimsy white ladies' boot box, thinking that in any case clothes cannot break. But to ensure it would be protected and arrive safely, I placed a talisman inside it.

Some weeks later a letter arrived from Pastor Vaughn:

"The parcel arrived damaged. It was held up at Customs. The officer told me to open it for examination. After I did, he looked through and found the little card with the Lord's name, that you had slipped between the clothes. He stared at the bold capital letters. "Oh, Jesus Christ is everywhere," he exclaimed, and then asked me: "Are you a Jesus Christ man?" and I replied, "Yes, Sir, I am."

"The customs officer hesitated. The contents of the parcel were valuable, and he could have charged a whole lot of duty. But then broke out in a smile. "That will be six dollars for you," he said.

"Do you realize, Sis, only six dollars! That's nothing compared to what I could have expected. The quality of those dresses would have cost much more, but for your Jesus Christ tag. Oh, Praise the Lord."

We wrote to each other for years, and then, as time went on and responsibilities increased, less so and more sporadically. Pastor Vaughn had become a Bishop. (But oh! the responsibility, Sis! It lies so heavy on my shoulders).

In June 1991 he was called to Guyana to minister to the people. A welcome service had been held in his honor under some old galvanized iron sheets propped up by some sticks and padded with coconut branches. Some people had come from as far as seventy miles away. Suddenly a heavy downpour began and people got wet.

"I was really shocked by their conditions. I found these people are so much poorer than those in Barbados. They had nothing, just the rags they wore."

Back in Barbados, the community responded generously to his plea for new and used clothing and "soon six barrels were lined up to be shipped to Guyana under the protection of that powerful, wonderful Name. Praise the Lord!"

A month later another letter informed me that he had returned to Guyana.

"The people are in such need. I live like they do. I wash in the river and drink the river water, like them. And I love being there."

In his next letter he wrote: "A kind person gave us a plot of land on which to build a church. Isn't that wonderful?"

In 1992 I went back to Barbados to visit the Vaughn family, and was made tremendously welcome. Pastor Vaughn and his wife moved out of their bedroom and gave it to me.

He smiled as told me: "The members of our church still talk about you, Sis. They will always remember you, because you washed the feet of the oldest lady in our congregation."

Not much had changed. The family lived with great simplicity. They both worked; Sister Vaughn as a maid in a tourist hotel. "They leave their clothes on the floor for me to pick up," she told me, completely matter-of-fact. Though he had become a bishop, *Pas Vaughn* had remained a humble brother as before. He still ironed his own shirt before going to church. Sister Vaughn prepared for me salads and vegetables, "food that Europeans eat." She was so kind, and I just loved being with them.

One evening, Pastor Vaughn said, "Would you like to pray with me, Sis?"

He took me into a quiet room, and as he prayed, his face became illumined.

"Did you know that angels came to talk to us tonight?"

It was with immense pleasure that I discovered, quite by chance, that on Independence Day, the 30th November 2006, the Fortieth Anniversary of the Independence of Barbados, Bishop Alfred Rudolph Vaughn's name was on the Honors list. He was given special recognition by the Government and honored publicly by being awarded the Barbados Service Star for having distinguished himself in his contribution to the community and the church.

As for me, thirty-four years have passed, and I have never experienced pain in my ears again.

IN THE EYE OF PARADISE

Pitch-black ten p.m. and terrified!

I stood stock-still facing the fat black spider (tennis ball size with legs stretched out) on the plain yellow cotton counterpane of the narrow twin bed of an English cottage on *Mahé*, a granitic island. Gusts of wind ghosted in and flapped the curtains eerily. Something at the front window, too, scratching. So this is what one got in Eden?

Back in Geneva I had reached the end of a cycle, and new possibilities had opened up. I found that suddenly I was free. My sons had gone out into the world; the life tasks had been accomplished, and for the first time I enjoyed plenty: of time and money. I had hoped my husband would join me; but islands, he said, were just not his thing. I was to be here alone.

This would be the first opportunity to travel in twenty-five years. Bar a few visits to local spots, I had never gone far. Now the whole world was not large enough for my dreams: I would find my paradise, and that is where I would go to live!

"Dowse the map for me," I had asked the old healer, knowing he could do so much more than most of his patients knew. I had seen my Uncle Joseph use a pendulum, so I was aware of its wide possibilities.

"I'm looking for places that will best match my energy," I told him.

While waiting, I dreamt a great dream that sucked me deeper and deeper into itself: I would take a magical trip; Greenland and virgin forests might even be in this too.

Within the week the dowser phoned me with his results.

"There are only three places you *can* go," he said, having dowsed the map of the world, with my vibes in mind.

"Just three?"

"Yes, and they are all volcanic islands! The Virgin Isles, Mauritius and the Seychelles."

It was the last that struck a chord. From then on the syllables of the Seychelles worked on me like a secret mantra. It was there I would find my Paradise. It was there that I would find the perfect match between who I was and the energy of the place.

One day it was my plane that swooped down over the whitewashed contours of the Seychelles archipelago of tropical islands that floated jewel-like in a turquoise, effervescent sea. The view from the air promised more than

I could ever have dreamed of.

Then the plane landed on *Mahé*, the tallest and biggest of the 115 islands that originated from volcanic action, and of which only 33 are populated. It bumped to a halt in stuffy, screeching traffic at midday at 30 degrees Celsius, just when everything was about to close. Not knowing where to go, and lugging my heavy blue vinyl suitcase with clammy hands, I took a bus to the city centre.

Mahé, I soon discovered, did not resemble my dream at all. It was far too big. 90% of the Seychellois population lives there. So this island was not *it*! The Tourist Office finally opened after its long siesta, and proposed a furnished cottage that was usually inhabited by an English lady, away for a year. I rented it for one week.

So here I was in one of my dreamed of islands - in the middle of the Indian Ocean, five degrees south of the Equator, 930 kilometers northeast of Madagascar, and feeling desperately alone.

Soon the warm day came to a close. Darkness blotted the world out, and cloaked the bungalow in black. Electric light life now began. Suddenly a long winged-thing flew across the room, heading for the ceiling. I followed it with gasping eyes only to find other inhabitants up there: at one end a large black spider, and at the other, a bronze house gecko eyeing it warily. The Seychelles had been isolated for millions of years (first discovered by the British in 1609).

That they held many ancient species was of no consolation to me at that moment. The southeast trade wind shook the shutters and shifted that flying thing. When I looked up again it was no longer in that crack in the ceiling. So where was it? A feeling of helplessness washed over me.

Then, odd scratching at the windowpane. Had a crab scuttled up from the beach below? The scary sounds rent the remnants of romantic visions that now fused with spiders, geckos and flying things, brown and longer than one's finger: surely not cockroaches *that* size?

I was free now, sure, but separated by worlds from anyone to call upon. Hadn't I always called one of *my men* to get that spider out of the bath? And been heard? First, my long-suffering husband and later, my reluctant sons. If it is true that most men can cook if they have to, it is *not* true that all women can handle their own spiders. Or even want to!

I slipped off my blouse and turned to lay it on the other bed; it was then that my eyes met his. The large, black spider I had spied on the ceiling (in the furthest corner from the flying thing) had shuffled down onto the twin bed; but would it stay there all night? A quick cowardly swat at it, with only half a glance. The Seychelles palm spider (*Nephilia inaurata*) can be seen on most telephone wires. The female (20 cm x 6 cm) is most impressive. Its web alone can have a diameter of 1.5 meters.

Here in the first leg of my dream, my worst nightmare had come true! I was surrounded by giant spiders. To top it all, I started a bellyache that was to keep me gated for the week.

A sudden heavy squall shook the banana trees behind the cottage and pelted the window panes. Cautiously, I, townswoman, pulled back the bedding to check: the sheets were virgin white and immobile. By the time I turned round, the other bed was clear. I looked for the spider's corpse; but it was nowhere to be seen. The spider had vanished without trace. Miserably I leapt into bed, eyes fixed on my sandals, to imprint their location for accurate recall in the dark; likewise branding the finger-feel of the switch of the bedside-lamp. Then I pulled the sheet over my face, and lay there motionless.

All of that without having had, as yet, the chance to buy provisions; nor to have lunch or supper. By two in the morning the wind had subsided and the rain had stopped. An uneasy silence wrapped itself around the fretting outline of darkly moving shapes. From below rose the muted murmur of the Indian Ocean.

Deep in the eye of the dream, in the granite heart of Eden, five degrees below the belt of the world, in search of Paradise. A weird palm-leafed spidery reality whispering in the night. Far from all things known, and very far indeed from a friendly hero, or even heroine. Taken unawares by visceral fear. Too old, I had thought, just to take off with a backpack; too young not to do it at all. Unaccustomed to sleeping alone, particularly with things-in-the-dark. Surprised suddenly to be over fifty. Eerie vigil.

Had a *gris-gris* been sent to get me? So soon?

Then distinctly, a faint meow.

As I opened the window to look, a wee black kitten leapt in from the porch. She had been waiting on the back of the tatty old beige armchair, trying to make herself heard. I poured her some milk and she lapped it up quickly. She seemed little more than a baby.

Then I lifted the bony little creature out again. I closed the window once more, searched for the spider, but could not see it though it had to be somewhere, examined the sheets for something alive, re-imprinted the exact location of my sandals and re-froze in bed. The joke was most certainly on me. My first "romantic night" was about to begin.

Next morning the screw pine and papaya tree stretched voluptuously into the brilliant sun. The banana trees, so ominous at night, now hummed with friendly life. The warm-hearted proprietress came over with breakfast: papaya, pineapple, toast and tea. The kitten appeared from nowhere and made for the tattered old beige armchair. A mere baby in plain daylight; a faded black, with faint streaks of dull, dusty brown; an old rag for a palaeolithic paintbrush. She jumped up on my lap and let herself be rocked to sleep. On the porch wall a saucer still held a few scraps of meat. There was someone who cared.

The maid came down with my breakfast on the second day. I asked her about the kitten. "Doesn't she belong to anyone?" She spoke to me half in French and half in Creole.

"The white cat, you know, the one with blue eyes, that's her mother. Haven't you seen her yet? I come to the bungalow early in the morning to feed her."

"The kitten is so tiny," I said.

"She's nearly six months old, though one wouldn't think so."

That afternoon the crisis began again; fear settled into me. There they were again, this time in full daylight, the odd sounds, somewhere near the kitchen door that opened onto the back garden. No, this was *not* a male ghost crab digging a burrow in my bathroom and vibrating his love songs with his large left claw; that much at least I could tell now from my travel brochure. Centipedes are silent, even the giant ones, and it couldn't have been one of the ancient tortoises in which these islands abound. So what was in my bathroom?

This was a special kind of sound, one I had heard before, I couldn't remember where. A sound that every mother knows and that moved me strangely, and rose and fell like music of forgotten days, in natural rhythm - now fast, now slow, now intermittent - replaying itself like a lullaby in the harmonics of my genetic code. Yet, filtered now through queasy quandary, visceral fear.

"Is anybody there?" I called, but only the soft sounds echoed back from the bathroom, touching my heart in a familiar way, without my finding words for it. Moments turned into minutes as I sat there motionless, knowing yet not knowing, called yet not answering, drawn into timelessness where fear was only a creation of the mind.

"Is anybody there?" I called again, but there echoed back only the immemorial circular, cellular sounds that have resonated in every mother's ear, and that rose and fell in natural rhythm - now fast, now slow, now intermittent, - till at last my resistance crumbled and I went to look. My footsteps did not alarm, nor slow down, nor did they arrest the activity in the bathroom, which became more and more familiar as I drew near, till I found her here: that same wee weanling that had scratched at the window earlier that day, now curled up on the bare floor, trying to find comfort by sucking a ragged strand of the fringe of the beige bathroom mat.

I picked her up and went to sit with her outside in the sun, caressing her gently till she fell asleep. The mite was just skin and bone; stunted like a sapling struck by a storm. Surely the ugliest kitten anyone had ever seen! For a while I held the tiny body and rocked her gently. Then the kitten slipped away and disappeared out of the back door.

That night I had a nightmare: I was lying at the bottom of the sea and a bunch of little fish was feeding off my left arm. The bite of their tiny teeth shook me out of sleep. I half-opened my eyes, barely focusing. The blue-green water was gone, but dark night was still in the room. Something continued to feast on my left arm. I had made a terrible mistake: this was, most definitely, not the oasis of my dreams.

Startled awake, and drunk with drowsiness, I raised myself drearily on my right arm and looked around: still in the same bungalow as the night before. But my left arm was still being chewed at under the blankets. With a shriek I threw the bedding back. The thing-in-the bed did not let go. Nor could I at first make out what it was. But with the click of the light switch, the nightmare ended as abruptly as it had begun. The baby kitten, curled up in the bed beside me, was sucking my arm, purring intermittently. I fell in love. Tender caresses, instant bond: murmured sweet-nothings, purring recognition. While I had shrunk away in spider-fright, the kitten had simply slipped into my bed.

I had never seen White Cat, the kitten's mother. But she made me furious. Reject *this* kitten? What kind of a mother was that!

But then, on the morning of the Third Day, I did see her on the porch wall, daintily picking at the meat the maid had laid out for her. She was sorely emaciated - though not for want of being fed, and nearly blind. "It often happens to those blue-eyed cats," the maid told me. My anger faded. Poor mother cat!

Suddenly I knew: I would have to do something about the kitten. Not that I knew what, but I'd made up my mind. So theory held that nothing could ever be undone, that no one could ever turn the clock back? Well, the mystics had it that *time does not exist*. So from that moment on the kitten's destiny had me to reckon with.

First, I gave the kitten nesting-rights in my bed, a not altogether one-sided affair. I was also trying to cure myself, not of maternal deprivation, but of feeling lousy. To this end I had embarked upon this journey with pockets full of Portuguese Oyster Powder, rich in trace-minerals - guaranteed to cure everything, including pregnancy, though this wasn't my problem just then.

That same day Heaven sent me a clue: one of my POP tablets dropped on the floor, and the kitten gobbled it up as if she'd been waiting for it all her life. I gave her several others. The next day a hint of sheen appeared on her coat, and with each passing moment I fell deeper in love.

I wanted to play with her; kittens can be such fun; but this one did not play: this was a wizened old baby never grown young. She barely left the armchair, except fleetingly to the edge of the lawn.

Finding a way to help the kitten was quite another matter. The oyster powder tablets polished her coat, but what else could I possibly do for her? At six months, she was a stunted little creature, whose mother had run out of milk too soon. I sent the problem up to the Only Place where it had a chance to be heard. Then I let go and stopped worrying.

On my Fourth Day the young man of the house came to visit. He took a liking to me and poured out all his woes. He was depressed, he said. He had had his horoscope done in India: changes, he'd been told, were on the way. This, however, did not resolve the problems he was having with his girlfriend, whom he desperately wanted to marry. I listened with a lifetime of living, plus the few skills in understanding that I had picked up on the way.

"Is she from a different culture?"

"Yes. She is a high-class Indian, whereas I

am Seychellois *(immigrants descended from France, India, Africa and China)*. I wait around at home for her to phone me and feel really miserable when she does not."

"You're sure about her?"

"Yes, but she does not want us to tell her parents, and I don't want to wait forever."

"You're too young to wait around at home," I said firmly. "Go out and enjoy yourself. Have some fun on your own."

The young man brightened. The next two days he came to the cottage again to consult me. Each time we spent hours in deliberation.

On the Fifth Day his mind grew clearer, my heart grew lighter, and the kitten became more alert.

On the Sixth Day the young man knew what he would do, though I still did not. The kitten's fur began to glow; so did I: we had become inseparable.

Then the first week was up. The young man said I could leave my blue vinyl suitcase at his house, while I was visiting the other islands. But I could not leave the kitten: not like that.

On the Seventh Day I exacted my fee.

"There's something I'd like you to do for me in exchange," I said.

"No problem!"

"Take the kitten up to the big house, to live with you. And give her the rest of my POP."

"No problem!"

At the end of the week I moved to *Praslin*, 44 km northeast of *Mahé*. It is the second largest island of the Seychelles, 10 km by 3.7. In spite of its gentle beauty, its primeval forest, its astounding Coco-de-Mer, and the gracious reception at my private residence, I cancelled my booking a few days later, and took the schooner across the six kilometers of sparkling sea to *La Digue*, 10 miles east of Praslin, and the smallest of all the Seychelles islands, only four square miles.

On this tiny island I found my way from the pier to the *Château St. Cloud*, a plantation house, run by Marston St. Ange, a descendant of an 18th Century French baron.

In those days it was *the* place to stay: an informal and comfortable alternative to a hotel. We all met for breakfast around the single refectory table, and again at night, when the Baron joined us. The Creole cuisine was excellent; even guests of the single hotel sometimes came to dinner, or moved over altogether. I was given one of the five rooms, and thoroughly enjoyed it. People arrived from many different places, many travelling, like myself, on their own.

Thus one day Jan and Mariette, a couple of

young Dutch biologists, turned up at the Château. They lived and worked on Cousin Island, trying to save the Magpie Robin (*Copsychus sechellarum*), once common, but now the 7th rarest bird in the world, from extinction. (By 1970 this species was reduced to 16 birds and had become extinct in the other Seychelles islands due to nest predation.)

I marveled at these Cambridge university scientists who were so excited because they had managed to breed five birds in captivity, and who told us, in confidence, that the news was not yet "out!" By investing all their time and energy, they were successful in pulling the species back from extinction. Jan and Mariette lived in a primitive hut, with only a mosquito net as protection at night from the myriad crawling things, some of which had no trouble slipping under the net. But this wonderful couple did not mind. Laughing, Mariette told me: "I am never sure whether what my hand is feeling in the dark is my husband, or a gecko!" At one with the birds she loved, her hair was streaked with many colors and tailed into a fine, long multi-colored strand, in brilliant plumage. In March 2004, her husband, now Professor, was nominated to the Chair in Avian Evolutionary Ecology in The Netherlands.

Time stands still in La Digue, where there is only one rough main road that suddenly ends and where other parts of the island can only be reached on foot or by bicycle. And where

Cycads, the oldest and most primitive of plants, grow along quiet paths and in whose reserve the jet black Paradise Flycatcher, known as *Veuve* (Widow) in Creole, of which there were only five pairs in 1997, has its only home in the world.

Just a little way from there, down the cobwebby path alongside of which midget bananas grew, past the cinnamon tree (from which I later bought two dollars' worth of bark), past the vanilla plants just in pod, past the boat-builders and the copra works, lay a beach of pure white sand guarded by massive granite boulders sculpted out of prehistory.

Photo ©Ania Mudrewicz

Granite rocks at Anse Pierrot, La Digue Island

On this tiny island my dream finally came true:
it was an experience of personal recognition.

Daily I went to bathe in the warm, turquoise
waters that sweep the fine white sands,
decorated with a ring of coral.

Daily I immersed myself in the timeless
presence of the huge granite boulders,
touchstone to both Heaven and earth.

For two weeks I was not anybody: I stopped
being a mother; stopped being a wife, stopped
being a professional, and stopped acting my age.
Each day I walked a little; then let the waves
wash over me.

For two weeks I played on the shores of life.

Photo ©Ania Mudrewicz

Ox cart tourist taxi trundling along Main Street,
La Digue

I was glad to be able to immerse myself in such peace – peace that was only animated from time to time by a group of tourists trundled along from the harbor by ox-cart and spilled out onto the beach for a brief swim, and then sharply recalled.

Nearly everyone got around by bicycle. As I became more energetic, I hired one, too, and began to explore the island. There were not many roads: three in all! At the end of the day, one would find a heap of bicycles stacked in front of the *Château*. But even in this place of magic and peace the abusers were present. Every morning a hard-faced woman who had rented a bungalow just down the road, sauntered by to sneak off with one of the bicycles that other people had paid for. One day I caught her in the act.

"No, you don't!" I declared vehemently. "Not mine!"

But she simply took someone else's and made off with it, saving herself the daily 25 rupees rental once more.

But beyond the trivia of daily life, lay the mystery of the granite boulders. Again and again I was drawn back to them, and daily I renewed myself in their presence.

Slowly I began to see why the findings of the old dowser in Geneva had sent me to volcanic islands.

Photo©Ania Mudrewicz

Granite rocks at Anse Source d'Argent, La Digue

I became aware that the emanation of these boulders had a strong revitalizing effect; they earthed one and at the same time connected one to the Heavens; anchored within time, yet they drew one into non-time.

Later I learned that granite is a very special stone with a good vibrational quality. It is used in sacred power spots such as Menhirs, Dolmens and Obelisks, and in Pyramid chambers. Some of it is slightly radioactive and can have healing properties. In fact, these have been birthed in the very heart of fire.

Some of the boulders at Pointe Source

d'Argent had curious shapes: one looked like a "turtle's head," another resembled a "big fort."

Soon newcomers arrived at the *Château:* and thus I met a South African doctor and his wife, who had been married for forty years, and were thinking of retiring on *La Digue.* She and I went out for early bicycle rides, and loved it.

Some time later there arrived an enterprising young woman, Ania, a world-wide explorer and Fellow of the Royal Geographical Society. For three days she whisked me along with her to discover the island. Our energetic explorations included an unexpected climb up to Island Peak, the highest point on the island. There we came upon the ruins of a house, but the French plum bushes were too thick to allow us to continue up to the highest ridge.

On the way down we enjoyed an unexpected encounter with a witchdoctor, a quiet, tall, lean man with white hair.

A witchdoctor is not a sorcerer. The *bonhomme de bois* (*bonnom, di bwa* in Creole) is in fact a seer, a traditional healer or medicine man, who in the course of a long and arduous training, has acquired a great deal of knowledge.

Photo © Ania Mudrewicz

The Witchdoctor

This meeting touched Ania profoundly. To this day she can still see clearly the witchdoctor's piercing blue eyes and curly, childlike hair. There was such stillness and grace in his demeanor. Ania is beautiful, has long blond hair, and is incredibly magnetic; there is something magical about her. Not surprising that Gypsies, fortune-tellers and healers are attracted to her. Our meeting with this tall, slender, quiet man brought back for her the memory of other such meetings: one witchdoctor in Madagascar and another in Colombia, as well as one who belonged to the Calazacon Colorado Indians and whom she had become very friendly with in Ecuador. One witchdoctor even asked her to live with him on his isolated island, and to become his wife. Here in La Digue, this seer too, seemed perfectly happy in this meeting, and allowed himself to be photographed with her.

By the time Ania left, I had gained a friend for life. She was as generous as she was beautiful. And it was she who made me a gift of the Seychelles photos in this book.

Soon the vacation came to an end for all, but me. The Baron excused himself and disappeared, leaving me in the care of the cook. So that evening, he invited me to sit in on a wake. The body lay in an open casket placed in the centre of the room, and many women kept vigil around it. The men played cards outside all night - to keep the evil spirits away.

The holiday in *La Digue* had served its purpose. It had enriched me and I was content. My quest had been fulfilled; I had found my rock.

Others, too, had found their perfect holiday spot. On the ferry to *La Digue*, I had met a middle-aged couple from Zürich. I noticed that all they had with them was one small bag.

"We come here every year," the wife told me. "Nine days are all we need to become completely restored."

I loved the place and there was much to explore. Day excursions to other islands were on offer, too. I took the one to Cousin Island Special Reserve (27 hectares or 0.27km²) a haven for a great variety of sea birds and endemic land birds. Up to 1988 it was the only island on which the Seychelles warblers (*Acrocephalus sechellensis*) occurred. Fascinating, too, were the thirty giant tortoises, some ancient. At the time, George, the eldest, was a centenarian, and in 2006 he was thought to be around 125 years old.

To preserve the island, only open to tourists five days a week from 10.00 a.m. to midday, and to keep it free from the accidental introduction of pests, there are strict regulations for visitors and wardens. (Cousin is the only island free of cats, rats and mice). All boats must anchor outside the island, and tourists are then transferred to the Cousin motor boat.

A handsome, tanned British scientist piloted us in and took us to the hut for a drink, where after we were taken on a tour by his fair-haired partner, a lovely English girl. After the tour, she told me that she desperately needed to talk to another woman. So we walked along the beach together. Like her partner, she, too, was a scientist. They had been quarrelling that day – about freshly baked bread. He was completely unwilling to take on the slightest domestic chore. She could not even rely on him to take the bread out of the oven for her while she was at work! And his being a scientist was absolutely no excuse!

We spoke about relationships, she and I, and before I left, she was smiling again. She had met *her angel* that day, right there on the island beach.

But the day came when I was so filled with the emanation of the island that I felt an urgent desire to leave La Digue. I had to get away.

"It is always like this," said the Baron. "It's the energy of this place. Visitors absorb it till they are completely saturated, and then all of a sudden they feel they must leave at once."

A full month after I had arrived in the Seychelles, I returned to *Mahé* to fetch my blue vinyl suitcase. I could not wait to see *my* kitten. But there was no sign of her. The proprietress gave me a warm welcome, but her son, the young man who had so often visited me to talk about his girlfriend, was not there.

"The mangoes are ripe now," she said in Seychellois French. "Pick some from the tree. Take as many as you like. And go to the cat-basket to see our brand-new kittens. They're just three weeks old."

I wasn't particularly interested in her big, fat cat, but the mangoes were perfumed rich ripe yellow gold. The thick juice slid down my throat, sidled down my neck and embalmed my hands. I couldn't stop eating. And yet I felt disappointed: the young man had not kept his word. He had not done anything for *my* kitten after all.

The proprietress interrupted my miserable trend of thought.

"My son is due back here any moment. He'll drive you to the airport," she said.

Then the young man arrived. He looked confident; stood taller than the last time I had seen him. He carried my suitcase to the car. I got in and waved good-bye to his parents. I turned to him.

"How did you get on with your girlfriend?"

"Oh, I was out the last couple of times she phoned," he said, looking very pleased with himself. "Gone dancing, having a really good time with friends. And last night she rang again to say she wanted to talk it over. But I kept my cool. Don't want her to think I'm hanging around waiting for her to call."

"And the kitten?" I asked at last. "Did you forget?"

"Oh, *her*! Of course not! The day you left I brought her up to the house, but I could not get her to stay. She ran straight back down to the cottage again."

My heart sank.

"So you weren't able to do anything for her, then?"

"Oh, yes I *was*! Every morning I gave her one of the tablets you left me"

I was delighted.

"But there is so much more to it than that!"

I couldn't wait to hear.

"When your kitten discovered our Persian Blue, she just snuggled in beside the three little kittens, and began to suckle."

"And the mother cat accepted the waif?"

"Oh! Yes," he said, as proudly as if he had done it himself. "And your kitten still comes up to our house every day to take her fill."

The young man started the car. I asked him to stop outside the cottage for a moment. I so wanted to see *my* kitten for the last time. But she was nowhere in sight.

But then, quite suddenly, she bounced into view: rounded out into a new fullness and much grown, *my* kitten was playing in the garden. Her fur glowed now, in this, her seventh month of life. The artist's careless splash had turned full sheen: dull, dusty brown glossed into gold gleaming on rippling midnight.

The kitten leapt and tumbled through the air in spirals of delight, chasing her tail, weaving in and out of her own loops. Nourished now on nectar, brimful with nose-in-belly warmth, the kitten had become boundlessly beautiful.

But she no longer responded to me when I called her. Nor did she come.

The holiday bungalow had been let again, this time to a tall, hefty woman, whose dyed blonde hair had black roots. When she heard us arrive, she emerged from the cottage jealously to guard her treasure and, as she looked on, I noticed that her harsh face softened.

The kitten had become *her* kitten.

ONE MAN'S SWISS JOURNEY

I recall his boyish smile, the beret tilted over his right eye - his strong, sinuous frame, the sap rising straight from the earth. Simmering beneath the surface, Michel was a burnished volcano.

Tall as a reed, proud and alone, he went out for his walk every day, whatever the weather. He was irresistibly magnetic; he drew the young and the not so young and turned them all into friends. Suddenly one would discover him, the centre of a little crowd. Wherever he was, beautiful women seemed to spring from nowhere; children ran to gather around him. And all this, without lifting a finger.

I remember him in snippets. Like the day my younger son, then seven, suddenly needed a daypack on a Saturday after the shops had closed, that first week, just after we had arrived in Geneva twenty-five years ago, and temporarily lived in Thônex.

"Go to see Michel," said my neighbor. "It's easy to find him; just go out the back gate and follow the little path through this field, till you get to a cottage in the middle of a meadow. It is only a few minutes from here. Say Maryse sent you."

"Not long afterwards my son returned with a small, well-weathered daypack, and a hamper full of strawberries.

"Michel told me to keep the daypack, Mum. Said he would not need it anymore."

"But who exactly is Michel?" I asked our neighbor sometime later.

"Oh, you haven't met him yet? He's the most marvelous person. Everyone knows him. Just go along and introduce yourself. His front door is always open."

We had barely been here for a week, when, just seven days later, and on a Sunday, my oldest son suddenly needed a compass. Where on earth could I find one?

"Go to see Michel," said the same neighbor as before.

And half-an-hour later my eleven-year-old came back with an old-fashioned compass and a hamper full of cherries.

"Michel told me to keep it, Mum. Said he did not need it anymore. And you know, he is an amazing person. You should visit him yourself."

And so the day came when I went to see for myself. Michel was on the front balcony, bent over his geraniums. As I walked through the creaking garden gate, he straightened his wiry, still youthful body and proffered a strong hand covered in earth. My right foot knocked into something lying on the cemented path.

"I always leave a saucer here for my hedgehogs. They come to feed early in the morning before anyone else is around. There are two of them. Quite tame."

He spoke as if he had always known me. His firm, generous handshake made me welcome. He adjusted his beret and looked at me from behind his misty glasses.

"So you are the boys' mother! Come inside and enjoy the chestnuts. I cooked them myself."

It was dark in the front room. The curtains were half drawn, but a ray of light spilt onto the plain wooden floorboards. He walked over to the kitchen, took out his penknife, and began to peel the chestnuts. There was a whole basin of them.

"Let's share them," he said.

In the solitude of being once more a stranger and having to speak a new language, Michel became my first friend. With him - no need to phone in advance. One was always welcome. No matter when one happened to arrive, he was always ready. His shopping invariably consisted of delicacies to share. He was in the habit of preparing feasts of raspberries, strawberries and cherries - in and out of season - and that day, had wild fresh walnuts that a friend had brought from her farm.

When Michel got to know me better, he began to tell me stories, and I gathered in the snippets like precious pieces of mosaic.

"I used to cycle to Italy," he began one day. "Whenever I was free I'd jump on my bicycle and take off. There were not so many cars on the road then, at the turn of the century. I was young and strong and never did need much money." Enigmatically his eyes looked into the past.

"On one of these trips I ran into a problem," he told me with a curiously young smile. "I had only one pair of jeans, you see. The ones I was wearing. And one day they split right down the middle! I always had a needle and thread with me, so I entered a little chapel in a side street, found a pew in the shadows and slipped out of my jeans."

With sure hands, Michel slowly lit his pipe.

"I was hoping to mend them before anyone came in. But I had barely begun when a nun emerged from the Sacristy and walked right up to me. "Let me do that for you, dear," she said, smiling. Then she took my jeans and walked off with them." He laughed. "But a few minutes later, she was back with the beautifully machined jeans."

I visited Michel often. Only the best and most exotic fruit or slices of *viande séchée des Grisons,* (dried beef smoked in the Alps) were good enough for visitors.

"Come, let's sit down inside," he said. "Going by your accent, you are English. So I'll make you a proper cup of tea. It's not many around here that know this, but there's a special way of making tea that I learned in England. It's the *proper* way."

This made me smile.

"Trying to get a decent cup of tea here in Geneva is maddening," I said. "The other day the waiter brought me a glass of warm water, accompanied by a flavorless teabag long exposed to the air. It barely colored the water. And they call that *tea* around here!"

He laughed. "I know what you mean."

Michel put the water on to boil, chatting the while, his front door open to the scented air of the summer garden. He poured the boiling water into the teapot without bothering to look at what he was doing, left the pot to warm, emptied it again when it was hot, and then measured out fresh tea leaves: one teaspoon per person, and one for the pot. Then he poured the boiling water over it.

"Your tea will be ready in exactly four minutes Ma'am," he said with a grin. "And now tell me all about yourself."

And in this way, the summer turned to autumn, and finally winter.

Finally the long winter ended, and springtime arrived once more. May was particularly glorious. Michel took me over to the corner cupboard and took out a tin.

"Smell this," he said, unscrewing the lid. "It's genuine beeswax from the South of France. I'm going to take everything out of this room tomorrow and will polish the floor."

"I could bring you an electric polisher," I volunteered. "I know where I can borrow one for you."

Michel looked at me in fierce disdain. "I don't believe in machines," he said belligerently. "Besides, it gives me something to do."

One day I turned up out of the blue. The front room was shaded as usual. Michel was busy in the sunny kitchen, his glasses steamed up.

"Come in," he said, "and enjoy some fresh pancakes with maple syrup. Friends from Canada send me a bottle of the genuine syrup every Christmas." We sat down together.

"Once I was travelling through northern Quebec," he began, "and out there in the wilds was a cabin in which lived a couple. They invited me in and offered me some bread with maple syrup and a glass of beer. "We tapped the sap ourselves," said the woman. Their shack was almost bare, save for a red cedar lute in one corner. The man picked up the instrument and pointed to the cracked soundboard. "No music now." Mute pain permeated the ensuing silence. "I'll try to have it repaired for you," I said. "Take it," said the woman almost inaudibly, and her husband's shoulders drooped. On my return, I finally found a luthier who said he could repair it. It was two years before I could go up north again, but then I took the lute back to the couple. You should have *seen* the joy in their faces!"

We were slowly getting to know each other. One day the smell of fresh beeswax permeated the cottage. "I love to get down on my hands and knees, and polish the floor myself."

But Michel never seemed to clean his glasses; they always looked smoky. "I can see you in that shaft of sunlight," he said one day. "You're wearing white. Besides, I know your voice."

Then, as unexpectedly as he had come into my life, Michel was gone. The next time I visited, his cottage was up for sale.

"Is he dead?" I asked a neighbor.

"Oh no! Michel was turned out. The cottage had belonged to the landlord's aunt. She died and he did not want to keep the property."

"So he just turned Michel out?" I asked, aghast. "At eighty-five?"

"Yes! And after he had lived there for fifteen years!"

"So how did Michel manage?"

"*Manage*?" she asked incredulously. "He had a new apartment in just three days."

"But it is so hard to find one in Geneva!"

"Michel has many friends, and it was a young woman who found him the new flat. There is also an older friend, Ninette, who comes regularly. They have known each other for over fifty years. It was she who organized his move and did many car trips herself. She will know where you can find Michel." I had met Ninette briefly in another context, so I called her, and she gave me his address.

Up an ugly, steep, cement stairway: sixteen steps. I found Michel's door open, as it always had been. Neighboring children filed in and out.

"I'll have some grapes for you next time, Julie," he called after one young girl. Fierce rage burned in me. Turned out at 85! Gone were the scented fields and the flowerbeds he himself had dug. Gone the peace of summer bees. Apartments now close together in a harsh, gray block. Concrete-amplified clamor.

"What happened, Michel?" I asked. He looked away through his misty glasses.

"*Life!*" he said, with a touch of bitterness. "But come to the balcony. Look, I brought my geraniums with me. Soon it will be too cold for them." He lifted the hessian sacking and brushed his hands over the plants. "They'll be glorious again, next spring," he said. He felt the individual stems. "Just look at *this one*. A real beauty! Gave me double blossoms for six months."

Michel had green fingers and was a gardener right to the depths of his soul, Ninette later told me. He could make anything grow.

"You'll find some fresh walnuts in the kitchen," Michel said. "Help yourself. Ninette brought them from her farm in France. She comes often and phones me every day."

The two-roomed apartment looked clean and fresh. A fine Elmwood sculpture stood in the entrance hall.

"You can touch it if you like," he said. I ran my fingers over the warm, smooth grain and texture of this undulating, natural form. "I carved it myself."

But Michel's spirit burned less brightly here. And yet, for me, being with him was like sitting in the warmth of a campfire on a moonlit night, under a star-pierced blue-black vault.

Implacably the concrete environment closed in on him. But he did not let himself be caged.

"I still go out for my walk every day," he said defiantly. "Nothing can stop me. I go whenever I feel like it, even if it rains. And I always go alone."

But there were small signs of self-neglect. From time to time I bumped into his friend, Ninette, usually as either she or I were leaving.

Each time I visited him he offered me something new.

"I had many beautiful old books once," he began, "but I left them all in the attic."

"In the attic? Where?"

"Oh, that was in Canada. On our farm."

He sank into a long silence, and gazed into the distance.

"I had fallen in love again," he told me, "madly in love. We were both retired and bought a farm. Every day we were out together in the orchards picking apples, as happy as children.

"Then one day she had to take a day trip to settle some business. That night the phone rang: there had been a car crash; a man's voice informed me that she was dead. Next morning I fled. Left everything behind me; never went back."

There was a stunned silence. But implacably Michel forced himself back to my presence.

"I taught in a boy's boarding-school once," he began with a smile. "Sunday mornings were chaotic. The boys were restless and rowdy, and the teachers dreaded having to look after them. We were also supposed to take a turn at preaching the sermon in Chapel on a Sunday! Just imagine: *Me preaching!*" He paused.

"So how did you get out of it?" I asked.

"Get out of it?" he laughed. "I refused to get into it! Told them I would take charge of the boys, on condition that no one ever broached the subject of a sermon, or asked me to preach again!" He grinned.

"And how did you manage the boys?"

"They were not bad kids; they were just bored. I began reading them an adventure story. Any boy who caused a disturbance was soon turned out by those who wanted to listen. When their curiosity was at its peak, I'd close the book. By the third Sunday all the boys were quiet. Rider Haggard's *King Solomon's Mines* was a winner!"

"It's easy to bore the pupils," he said. "But I took the boys out in the middle of the night and had them measure the plants to see whether they grew faster in the moonlight or in the light of the sun. I never had any trouble with them."

From time to time Michel would sink into silence, then murmur, "*C'est long!* It goes on and on!" And the words would resound like a mournful refrain.

One day I found the front door open. Michel was rummaging in a drawer. "I've had a letter from my son," he said. "It's in this drawer, somewhere."

"You have a son?"

"Oh yes, he is over forty now. He visits me once a year. I also had a wife once. I never asked for a divorce; just walked away when it was over!" Then Michel changed the subject.

"When I was little, we lived on a farm above Bonmont. It was situated below the ruins of the *Vieux Château*, an old castle destroyed in 1476 during the Burgundian wars. From there one could see our farm, and also had a magnificent view down to the lake, as well as to the Mont-Blanc. It was idyllic."

The walls of the dungeon were still erect when Michel was a boy, though they have since disintegrated and are now overgrown. Now there is a didactic path (*La Ballade à Béatrix*) through the forest to the ruins. On the way up to the esplanade, sixteen information boards describe the last episodes of the life of the castle as it was in the ancient novel about the legend of Béatrix. "And do you know," Michel continued, "the story goes that a woman was found embedded in one of the dungeon walls."

Michel looked at me with evident satisfaction. "Being a child on that farm was like being raised in paradise. We had a lot of horses. When I was three, I'd walk freely under the legs of the horses and tickle their bellies. I don't know how they put up with me! But not one of them ever kicked me.

"I love animals," he continued. "When I was ten, I went to visit the elephants in Geneva. The *Cirque Knie* (Knie Circus) would leave them in the *Parc des Eaux-Vives*, a vast domain with a lake constituted in the 16th century, but then only a large enclosure. There were six elephants, and I wanted to be with them. There was no attendant, so I simply climbed over the fence."

"What happened then?"

Michel flashed me his boyish grin. "One of the elephants picked me up and put me on his back. He took me for a ride all around the enclosure, and then set me down at the very place he had picked me up to start with."

Founded by the Knie family in 1803, and performing under a big top since 1919, the tradition of the Swiss National Circus Knie continues to this day. I wonder if any of their elephants today are the grandchildren of the elephants of Michel's youth.

One day Michel talked about his friend, Ninette.

"I met her in Canada, when her husband was a lecturer at University. It is thanks to her that my flat is so well organized. She takes care of everything. See that painting hanging above my bed - (mysterious green trees casting shadows over a pond) - Ninette painted it. In Quebec, all three of us would go riding in the Boreal forest. The scenery was glorious."

Later Ninette told me, "Afterwards Michel would write poems. They were sublime."

And she added, "He was my painting and pottery teacher."

On my next visit, Michel got back to the subject of elephants.

"I was in Frankfurt one year, and a circus had come to town. So I walked over to the elephants. They looked unhappy and depressed. I leaned over the enclosure to the nearest one, and stroked his trunk. "You're not from here," I said, and a quiver went through the group as I spoke. The other elephants approached and brightened up. "So I was right!" he said. "You speak French!" Elephants can also feel lost in a foreign country, you know."

Then Michel sank into silence, broken only by that solitary refrain: "It just goes on and on."

I was on Tram 12 as it stopped at Plainpalais (at the other end of the tram route) when I saw a familiar figure plant his cane firmly in the doorway at the front entrance. It was Michel, whom I had not seen for months.

"I'll get off here with you," I called out to him, shocked at the state he was in.

"I know your voice," he said, without looking at me. I took his arm and we both got off.

"What on earth are you doing *here*, Michel?"

"I had to get out," he growled. "I couldn't stand it any longer. It's like being buried alive. I didn't care where I went and just got on the first tram." We stepped into a café and sat down.

"I've had enough," he thundered. "It just goes on and on and on!"

I sipped my coffee, silent, helpless, drawn into the tempest.

"I miss my two hedgehogs," he complained. "I always left a saucer of food out for them. I loved living in that cottage. Early every morning a blackbird would tap at my window and I'd feed it."

"C'est long," he said. *"C'est long."*

Michel had not shaved. He looked shrunken; his shoulders had drooped.

"Getting back upstairs after shopping is easy," he said. "I just count the steps on the way up. But once inside my flat I cannot tell whether I'm heading for the front door or the back. It's like living inside a large round clock, but I don't know which way the hands are turning."

Nor could Michel ascertain whether it was day or night. At three one morning he walked out of his front door and fell down the jagged, concrete steps. Hours later a neighbor found him, bleeding, bruised and blue with cold. He took Michel to hospital, and left him there.

"I sat there and waited, and waited, but no one came. Too busy, they were," he raged. "Much too busy for me! I waited *three* hours. Then I'd had enough. I walked out, took a taxi home, washed and went to bed. They're not ever going to get me again! You know, I had a car accident once in Canada. When I came round, I was in a hospital. Well, I found my clothes and escaped. You won't catch me in a hospital again!"

More often now, Michel would repeat:
"It just goes on and on and on!"

And the silence that followed would engulf us both in its night.

When Michel could no longer walk about freely, Ninette hired a young Indian woman to live in. Sunita was graced with the purity of untouched innocence, and was angelically beautiful. Her long black hair, braided in a single plait down her back, reached to her waist. Fresh as a fresh young olive tree, and radiant in her orange-red silk sari, she took care of Michel with gentleness and love.

One day I felt a sudden urge to visit Michel, and found N1nette there, extremely stressed. It was Sunita's day off. Michel could not be left alone.

"Could you stay here for a couple of hours?"

It was shortly after his 90th birthday. I read him an African folk tale: Kumongé, the Magic Tree. Suddenly he drew himself up in bed and said, "I lived in Africa once." And he continued the tale in a deep, sonorous voice, in some African tongue unknown to me, rhythmically, powerfully, as might a young warrior.

A few days later Michel died peacefully, in his own home.

Later Ninette told me more. "Michel's eyesight had begun to deteriorate in Canada. That is why he returned to Geneva. But he had one good eye. Later this eye, too, had to be operated on. We took him to the best eye surgeon. The operation partially restored his sight, but only for a while, for he had glaucoma. Then that eye also gave way."

"Did you find it difficult to look after Michel in those last few months?" I asked.

"Oh no! *Ça m'a fait vivre!* It made me feel fully alive."

For both of us his friendship had been a great privilege.

Michel's departure was celebrated in St. George's Chapel in Geneva, with lilies and colored wreaths. He drew many people. Some huddled in front; others straggled here and there. Beautiful young Sunita sat alone, at the very back. The University Choir sang. Mozart's Requiem filled the chapel. And many mourned Michel.

Twelve years have passed. Ninette is now eighty. Her face lights up and her voice glows as she reminisces.

"You mean he never told you?" she exclaimed one day. "Michel led a most amazing life. All the most important people were in touch with him, and he corresponded with men of fame. But he kept no records; left no records. That is the way he was - a wonderful person and a free spirit." Her husband, likewise eighty, nodded in agreement.

"Michel despaired when he found himself going blind. He loved life passionately, and clung to it. He could not let go. When he was eighty, he still insisted on climbing up the cherry tree on my farm to pick the cherries. He was interested in everything - even the people in the street. Generosity itself, he gave away virtually everything.

"His curiosity was boundless. When he was a child, they lived near the French border. So, on his way back from school, he would go to the inn to watch the smugglers who came in for a glass of hot wine. The little inn would be crowded. But there was room on the top landing, and they let him stand there and watch. "There were always such beautiful women," he had later remarked."

As her memories sharpened, Ninette continued enthusiastically, "You know, when Michel was a child, a raven would accompany him to the village school every day. This raven did not like his father, and when he was not looking, it would quickly unpick his shoe laces.

"Michel loved to go down to the lake and explore; he loved to hide and watch the otters.

"When he had completed his studies, he taught in Neuchâtel for a while. Later he came to Geneva.

"His mother was French and Michel later married a French woman. For a wedding present he was given an extraordinary cat. They slaughtered a pig, made *le boudin* (black pudding) and invited the neighbors to the festivities. But his in-laws wanted the cat out of the way, and locked it in the cellar for three days. Excluded thus, and thoroughly offended by the time it was finally let out, the emaciated cat refused to touch the meat from the wedding feast."

"And what happened to the couple?"

"They were too different for the marriage to work."

The pieces of the enigma were falling into place. I began to perceive Michel's life more as a whole.

"When he was in Canada, Michel worked as a private tutor in a college. During the 1920s he introduced pottery to the *École Technique* in Shawinigan, a city located on the Saint Maurice River in Quebec, and continued to work there for the next decades.

"In the holidays he would take off to the North and there he would hunt and fish, and light a campfire. Michel would go to live outdoors as often as he could." I was touched by her sharing.

"Michel was a veritable force of Nature. But his blindness turned him into *un grand revolté*, a man enraged at his fate."

In fact, Michel had tried to avoid Customs altogether! But he had rarely shown me that side of himself. As a friend, he had been a tower of strength. I had arrived in Geneva a stranger. In moments of solitude, Michel had been a companion. In moments of sorrow, he had made me laugh. To the children he became a friend. For me he was the boundary marker in the crossing from one culture to another, one life to another. Above all, Michel bequeathed me an enduring example of courage.

LATE CROSSINGS

GETTING THROUGH CUSTOMS

THE RING

Shadowy brooding possesses my soul. Clouds hover over the rose garden. Where does promise dwell?

A story overshadows me, invades. I move aside uneasily. What will this story tell?

Tightness grips my stomach. It spreads upwards, hits between the ribs. I am back in constriction. Back behind the Iron Curtain, back in my hometown. I have just returned alone from the mountain village to which my father packed us off in such haste this summer. I am back from the Mountain of Wolves.

It was there one winter, when the village was covered with snow that my father was out with his daughters. It was there, when the *Berg* was white with snow, that a rabid hound came racing towards them, gnarling with foam. And it was there that winter that my father simply turned to face him, and with his good left hand tightly fisted, bashed him on the snout.

In the town below the foreign soldiers had moved in and were looking for girls. I child, am six or so.

One does not get to this village by car; and the train goes only part of the way. But one gets there in an open horse-drawn carriage that also serves to carry hay. (Three hours are long on the rickety plank that is the seat).

The village is primitive; open drains run alongside the cottages down the rough stone street. The peasants wash their vegetables and their feet in the kitchen sink (so my Mother used to complain) and the water trickles out lazily to the side of the road. Bread is baked in an oval outdoor oven. Cows are hand-milked. Down in the coolness of the cellar the peasants leave the rich full milk to curdle slowly in deep earthenware pots. Later it turns into *Sauermilch* with chunky iceberg islands that float in whey. (There is a long ladle for this). Eating is simple; we get a soup plate full of this and a hunk of black bread. I love this. When we're extra lucky we get a slice of bread thickly spread with goose fat, crystal-topped with sugar. In those days, I think this is wonderful.

There are several small children; we make a little band, in fact. We run around barefoot like mountain goats. Town-child, I step gingerly at first, as on jagged glass. But by the end of the summer I skip along tough-soled and agile as the others over the rough, sharp stones of road. The village children are clever, I think. Especially Peter. He teaches me how to make a boat. We send the paper boats with their straw masts floating down the open drains. They have shorn my hair that summer and put me in rough-cloth shorts. The boys are lucky in that outdoor way; a tree is all they need. But I have to lag behind and hide. I am the only girl.

Something has happened between us up in that mountain village; something deep and true.

"Papa," I tell him excitedly, back in my hometown, "Papa, I am going to marry Peter. But he has no shoes. Will you buy him a pair, from me?"

My father is very thin and tense. He looks at the floor; then says something or other.

But something has happened deep inside me that summer; something for which I have - as yet - no name. In the shadowy past of a little girl's knowing resides a memory that now bolts out of my esophagus, too long held captive. A memory that now wants to be owned.

Outside, the soldiers trampled the streets, hungry for something. The World was then in War II.

Fee, Fi, Fo, Fum!

But where had all the lasses gone?

Inside, I followed my own dream.

"Mama, I need a ring," I told her urgently, back home alone.

Mama was very beautiful and had many necklaces and rings in those days, a whole box full of them. Surely she could give me one?

"I need a ring *for me*, my Mama," I repeated, and did not think this was a problem.

"So you want a ring?" had said my scraggy middle sister back there in the village, when I first dared to put it into words.

Then, in those war days, she was just fifteen.

"A ring, you say? Just come with me!"

And my sister took me out to the road where the homecoming cows were crossing. A few paces behind them walked a peasant leading a thickset bull with a long pole. The clip on the end was hooked into a copper ring in the bull's nose.

"See that bull?" she said sharply. I stared at her, unable to grasp the point. She glared at me from above her too-thin neck, while her forehead puckered into a desperate frown.

"See that bull?" she repeated. "See his nose? Right? Well, you can have a ring just like his!"

Her jibe sank down my esophagus as I drew in my breath sharply, and slipped deep down inside me like an icy, king-sized marble, that has lain there ever since.

Something happened in my heart that summer; something for which I had as yet, no name. And when I got back home, I bothered my mother and I bothered my father, till despite those jibes, I got my ring. We went to the big polished jewel-box and my mother and my father and I bent over it. Mama's fingers pushed the rings this way and that till they rustled and clinked against each other. At last, she picked one up - too big for me by far - and held it up to the light.

"You can have this one," she said.

It was Papa who had the ring remounted, little-girl finger sized. It took what seemed a long, long time, but then, at last, it homed proudly on my left fourth finger.

But no sooner was it given, than again it was taken: for the time had come to leave, with only a suitcase or two.

Papa said, "You can't take that ring with you. It's out of the question!"

And that little-girl's embodiment of dream was left behind, though the icy, king-sized marble slipped out with her.

Fifty years passed. Inhabited again one day by that strange, uneasy brooding, I set out on foot along the tramlines into the centre, dreaming of a ring, without knowing why. It was not my birthday, not an anniversary, not even Christmas, but something was simmering inside me. Then the sun broke through the clouds, and shone brilliantly as I, woman, followed the solitary trail, heart set on a Fire Opal.

I had pursued that trail tentatively ten years before; then too, without knowing why. It had led me to a wholesale jewelry shop whose large showcase displayed a rich array of rubies and sapphires straight from the owner's own private mine in South America. But that was where my adventure had ended, then.

Now, a decade later, I wanted to go back

there. A faint memory drove me to the wrong passage and up two flights of stairs, only to bring me to a halt in front of a closed door with a drab sign: *MOVED*.

But the scrappy, hand-written address beneath it led me to an altogether different jeweler's shop, one I had never seen before: small and discreet, with very little on display. There was just enough room for one person behind the counter, and a leather chair in front. I lingered outside long, looking in. Two heads were bent over a necklace; then the client left.

I entered, slow motion, as in a dream. Timidly, at last, "Do you have a Fire Opal to show me?"

"No, but what do you want it for?"

I could not say, really. I did not know. But he began to talk to me about gemstones and their powers, most passionately so.

"I believe that each stone has its own vibration and its own power. Some gems can even heal. Don't you think so, too?"

I smiled in response. He stared at me, then added: "But you know about vibrations, I see."

He fished under his collar. "Look, here on this chain I wear a square of jade and an amber dragon. They protect me, keep me healthy, and bring love and victory."

"Where are you from?" I asked him.

"Italy," he replied proudly. Then he looked at me intently, "So you're after an *opale de feu!* Is it for a pendant? No! For a ring?"

162

"For a ring."

"What do you want to pay for it?"

"I don't know."

"Just leave this to me," he said, the Italian in him rising to the occasion.

Seven weeks went by and I forgot that trip into town. Then one day at work, the phone rang. It was the jeweler.

"The opals you ordered are here."

"The *opals* I ordered? But I only asked for one!"

"Well, I got you three."

"Three?"

"A young woman brought them in for you today. They're free."

"Free?"

"But this is Geneva! What do you mean by free?" He just laughed.

"I mean," he said, "you don't have to pay for them!"

I couldn't wait to get to the jeweler's shop after work. Looking exceedingly pleased, the Italian welcomed me with a broad smile. He unwrapped three rough Fire Opals, like orange shards. The summer sun lit them fiercely, revealing flashes of color that played and changed. Their orange glow filled me with warmth, brimful. But I felt perplexed.

"What young woman came in?"

"Actually," he began, "a young man came in

first. The traveler kind with a backpack. Laid his grubby handkerchief on the counter and unwrapped a Fire Opal. Brought it back from Mexico or somewhere. These kids come in here all the time. But I told him I had a client for whom I needed three, and turned him away. He must have gone and talked about it. Half an hour later a young woman walked in. Same kind: long dress and backpack. "I'm *giving* you these," she said, "for the lady who needs them for their vibrations or something." So you see, I wouldn't dare to make you pay for them!"

I picked the most beautiful of the three Fire Opals for the ring.

Photo ©Emmanuel Power

The Fire Opal ring

Suddenly there was a lot to discuss: the shape, the cut, the setting, to polish it or not. Then it was sent to the workshops: first the lapidary, genuine artisan of the old school (now not many left, the jeweler said); and then the setter for mounting.

"Keep these for earrings," he concluded, handing me the other two Fire Opals.

It took seven weeks before he summoned me: the ring had arrived. Oval now and translucent, orange fire danced in the sun as I held it up to the light. Its burnished glow suffused me. Then I, half-century woman, slipped it on my finger, and instantly turned six.

"What did you really want the ring for?" the jeweler asked quietly.

But I had already slipped out.

There had been no promise, but what life had once taken, it now restored. And the memory was made beautiful.

IN SEARCH OF THE BIG BLUE ELEPHANT

M y lifelong friend, Hélène Nixon-Christeller, has died. She has outlived many members of her family, and most of her friends.

Most of us knew her as Chris. She was born on December 22, 1915 to missionary parents in Morija, then Basutoland, now renamed Lesotho. Her father, Charles Christeller, (born in 1868) was a French pastor sent by the Paris Missionary Society to Lesotho in 1892.

But it was at the University of Natal, Pietermaritzburg (SA) that I first met Chris. Then she was forty, and I sixteen. She was the Warden of the Women's Residence, and my father literally handed me over to her care.

Half a century later, I was called upon by *La Fondation Lambrechts*, a home in Paris, to help them sort out Chris's papers and affairs. It was then that I discovered the memoir of her youth in a series of articles she had published between 2000 and 2002 in their *Journal*.

But what came as a complete surprise, was to find among her papers, some handwritten notes on her dreams that she had been noting for years and had classified according to Freud's *Interpretation of Dreams*. These she used as the basis for two lectures in which she encouraged fellow residents likewise to note their dreams.

To honor her memory and to remain true to her spiritual and historical foundations, we shall frequently use Chris's own voice.

Beneath the shadows of ageing, three remarkable dreams revealed the grandeur of her spirit.

Below is a translation of her first dream.

I am walking along my favorite beach on the edge of the Indian Ocean and stop on the top of a sand dune that rises above it. At my feet lies a little beach of fine white sand. It is a beautiful sunny day. The sea is of an indescribable color, a wonderful mixture of blue, green and white; a sort of turquoise, milky and glittering. (...). There are hardly any waves, but one can sense a swirl beneath the surface of the water. These waters are alive.

About twenty sun-tanned bathers, all of them Whites, are having great fun, swimming, diving, and tumbling this way and that. I can hear snatches of conversation; joyful laughter. On the right, three elephants are frolicking in the water amidst the bathers. They are of a delightful pale green. They seem to be adolescents, with gaunt flanks and exaggeratedly long thin legs. (...). Their movements are awkward (...) but their youthfulness makes them endearing. These, too, are having a whopping good time, letting themselves fall in the water, tumbling over one another, toppling each other over. To the left of the group of bathers, a lone adult elephant, of the same delightful pale green, begins to emerge from the water calmly and move towards the beach. The whole scene is one of joy and happy, carefree holidays, (…) and I feel the depths of happiness. (…) It is wonderful to see them like this, the bathers and elephants, accepting each other completely and intensely enjoying life.

(…) But what would happen, I ask myself, if they got into a rage and charged? Then the bathers would not have the slightest means of defending themselves.

End of the dream.

The meaning of this dream could not have been clearer. Even in my dream I knew that the elephants were a symbol for the Africans amongst us. For me the joyful scene represented an idyllic situation in which Whites and Blacks live together in freedom and harmony.

However, deeper reflection made me divine a future in which vengeance and retribution could no longer be contained. So this dream represented for me an ardently desired ideal, as well as the harsh reality to come.

Chris's clear, fluid handwriting drew me back. How often through life I had received her wonderful, encouraging letters.

It had been five decades since I had first met Chris at the University of Natal (South Africa) where she taught French in Pietermaritzburg, and her lectures were a delight. Her clear, musical voice was enchanting. She started us on Saint Exupéry's *Le Petit Prince,* and I can recall it to this day.

At the Women's Residence I was allocated a small single room with murky dark green walls. I found them oppressive, so I asked Chris if I could paint them white. She was surprisingly open-minded, and gave me permission. In those days this was a very unusual thing for a "White girl" to do. And when the African man servant saw me with my roller and tin of paint, he could not believe his eyes! Well into old age, Chris reminded me of it one day in Paris at the home: "You were a very enterprising young lady," she said.

My father was delighted to discover that Chris belonged to the Morija community of French-speaking missionaries who took in students during the holidays. So at the first opportunity, he sent me to Lesotho for a fortnight in such a family. Chris was there, too, and was to become a lifelong friend.

My greatest joy was getting around on horseback. The small, sturdy, sure-footed Sotho ponies, up to fourteen hands high, had been introduced by the missionaries, and were essential in the steep mountains and gullies, as well as for carrying the grain to the mill.

Sotho Ponies

One day, Chris and I went riding, intending to reach a nearby village. But on the way, the sky darkened, the clouds broke and a downpour began. Wet and bedraggled, we dismounted.

The village Headman welcomed us in Sesotho, which Chris spoke fluently, and showed us to an empty hut. Its only furnishings were two assegais on the circular wall. A woman brought us two colored Basotho blankets and two large safety pins.

We peeled off our soaked clothes and feeling like naughty schoolgirls, each of us hung our bra on an assegai to dry. Then, with our blankets pinned around us, we were given a hot drink.

BASUTOLAND. — A Native Village.   Phot. Dr. G. Hertig

A Sotho Village

This was to remain a little secret between us, and Chris never forgot it. Many a time, as we both grew older, and she grew frailer, her eyes would light up with youthful gaiety, and right out of the blue, she would suddenly come out with: "Do you remember the assegai?"

Another thing Chris did was to ask one of the mission children to take me to see the dinosaur footprint. I had never seen one before, and seeing this track left behind by a prehistoric giant 65 million years before, thrilled me and altered my awareness of the duration of time.

Many other dinosaur footprints were discovered in the 20th Century in Lesotho by the Reverend Paul Ellenberger who held two B.Sc. degrees, one in paleontology.

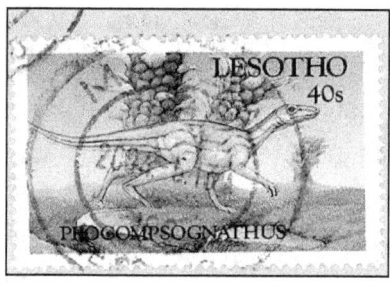

The stamp shows a Procompsognathus dinosaur.

Chris took me to the Morija church, which the missionary builder, François Maeder, together with other constructions, had taken ten years to complete.

The Church of Morija

The church of Morija was inaugurated in 1858, attacked and partly destroyed by the Boers, but rebuilt, and stands to this day.

From a letter addressed to Chris in 1995

In 1942 Chris married Desmond Nixon, a Methodist minister. He had contracted TB in Ireland and had been sent to South Africa in the hope that, away from the damp and pollution of cities, the climate would help. Chris knew of his illness before she married him and they had a wonderful relationship. During their ten years together she devoted herself to being a minister's wife and looking after her husband. Desmond died in December 1952. Widowed at the age of thirty-seven, Chris never married again.

It was not long thereafter that her cousin, Sam Germond (the School Secretary for the Lesotho Evangelical Church) invited Chris to join him on a three-week horseback tour to inspect the schools in the Malutis.

Chris (left) with her cousin, Sam and Jacobo

Sotho life in the Mountains

Chris narrates: "There is no road across the mountains, except for the first few kilometers. So one has to cross them on foot or on horseback, or in a small two-seater plane that can only land in a few places. So the three of us, Sam, I and Jokobo, the Mosotho who looked after the horses, set out. The vegetation in the mountains was surprisingly so much more abundant than on the plain. It was hot, and when we passed a little river, the Kétane, which turned into a little waterfall at the bottom of which lay a deep pool, the temptation to plunge into the icy water was irresistible – as was that of sunbathing on the big, flat rock thereafter. But at 3,400 meters altitude, I was covered in blisters in no time, and to ride thereafter was sheer torture." (*Notre Journal* of March 2002)

Chris loved the nights. "Sam slept in his tent, and Jakobo outside to ensure that the horses did not stray too far. As for me, I slept in my sleeping bag, thinking with pleasure of Robert Louis Stevenson's "Travels with a Donkey in the Cevennes," and of the joy and peace that such a night under the stars can bring."

Some time thereafter, Chris began to work. Her first job was that of junior lecturer in French at the University of Natal, Pietermaritzburg (S.A.). This led to a scholarship to the Sorbonne, and her year of study in Paris was brilliantly successful. As a student, Chris lived in a small, primitive attic, but she loved every moment of being in Paris, and wrote the most enthusiastic letters. Then, with her new diploma, she returned to South Africa, to begin teaching French at Rhodes University in Grahamstown (Eastern Cape). She made innumerable friends and worked there until she retired.

In October 1978 I visited Chris in Grahamstown, but as she was busy lecturing at the University and thus not free, she had rented a cottage for me at The Port, Mossel Bay, where she joined me in the week-end. The beach there was very rocky and I was somewhat nervous about getting into the water, but. But when Chris arrived, she Chris plunged in fearlessly, as if the sea and the rocks were her second home. Her nephew told me that her husband had been posted there, and that she had often gone down to the harbor to swim.

Chris wrote me wonderful letters from wherever she lived. After she retired in Grahamstown, and after much soul-searching, she decided to leave South Africa and move to Paris, in order to help her ageing older sister and her brother-in-law, both of whom were seriously ill. But some years later, when her sister had become too handicapped to be able to continue living at home, Chris was faced with a major decision. The retirement home would not admit her sister, unless she arrived with a personal nurse to provide the extra care. Chris had already nursed her husband, her mother, bed-ridden in her nineties, and her older sister. Now, still in the prime of retirement, she volunteered to be that nurse. Freedom crumbled into dust.

"It is like entering a long, grey tunnel," she wrote to me after the first month in the home.

This saddened me, and I would visit her whenever I could and through the long years to come, we kept in touch and her letters proved to be an inspiration to me. "I want to live victoriously," her next letter announced, as she determinedly overcame her first distress.

Visiting her in her little studio in the home was always a pleasure. She would provide biscuits and tea, and turn my visit into a real treat. We had fascinating conversations, and time always slipped away too fast.

From time to time weird things would happen, too. At four-thirty one afternoon a distraught woman from a few doors down, knocked at Chris's door. "Is it time to go down to dinner?" Five minutes later she knocked again and repeated the same anxious question; and continued this procedure every few minutes. It looked like an absolute farce, and I was in stitches. "It is not funny," said Chris. "Since her husband passed away, the poor soul has lost her mind."

Finally even *her* patience ran out. "Go back to your room at once, Madame," Chris said firmly as the woman popped in for the fifteenth time. "And stay there until the bell rings."

There was a time when Chris had such uncontrollable back pain that in spite of herself she would burst into tears at dinner. To spare the others, she wanted to go to her room. However, there was a strict rule; residents were not allowed to leave the table until the end of the meal, no matter what!

My visits provided light relief. At dinner time we would be placed at a private table and could enjoy each other's company. The cuisine in the home was good, and the wine helped.

One day in the lift, Chris introduced me to a short, portly gentleman, Monsieur l'Évêque. I could not see his ecclesiastical ring, but bowed respectfully. Chris was barely able to suppress her laughter. "He's not a bishop!" she said, as soon as we were out of earshot. "Lévéque is his *name*!"

Time ran away with us, and by evening, Chris was all for keeping me in her room for the night. "It would be great fun," she said. "But what if we're discovered?" She laughed. "Did I ever tell you," she said, "about the time I got locked out of a hostel in the Canton Vaud? Well, I had come from Paris to visit a relative in a small village, and had booked into an inexpensive hostel run by religious folk. One had to be in by ten, and they were very strict. Well, I was sixty-seven by then! When I got back at 11:30 p.m. and found the door locked, I simply climbed in through the window!"

Here in Paris now and long after the front

door of the home was locked, Chris sneaked me out at midnight, as young in spirit as when I had first met her. The hot water bottle strapped to her back had begun to slip. "It's ridiculous," she said just as I was leaving, "but this is the only way I can stand the spasms."

In the home's *Journal,* Chris briefly outlined the history of Lesotho. "It is a little bigger than Belgium and encompasses a number of different tribes welded into one people by the genius of Moshesh. Virtually naked in a leopard skin, armed with an assegai (a primitive lance) and a beef skin shield, he became the Chief of the nation at the age of thirty-four and one of the greatest figures in the history of southern Africa.

The above design, found on the air letters of the time, is the emblem of Lesotho: a shield with the crocodile (*kuena* in Sesotho), the totem of Moshesh's clan, an assegai and a knobkerrie. Below this is the motto: peace, rain, prosperity.

"At the beginning of the 19th Century, the tribes inhabiting the region that today is called the Orange Free State fled before Chaka, the Zulu King in Natal, who with his hordes of Zulus, massacred the inhabitants and stole their cattle. The Boers lived around the Cape of Good Hope, but they fled from the English – who were governing the Cape – travelling in ox wagons to the north. This came to be known as the Great Trek.

Travelling by ox-wagon (F. Christol)

"They met some Sotho and other tribes that had been fighting one another, often pressed by Zulu tribes coming from northern Natal. When they arrived in the regions devastated by the Zulus, they found them rather deserted. But not for long, for those left sought the protection of Moshesh, King of the Basotho (1786 - 1870).

"So for many years, Moshesh had to battle not only with invading Zulus, but also with the Boers who, crossing the Orange River, were establishing themselves in an area previously occupied by African tribes. The tribes that managed to escape the Zulus took refuge in the sparsely inhabited Maluti. Their fields had been devastated, their cattle stolen and starvation threatened. Hunger turned them into cannibals. To survive, they began to eat their own, starting with those who were too weak to defend themselves. Thus Moshesh's own ageing grandfather was captured and eaten by cannibals. However, Moshesh did not take up arms against them, but looked upon them as the living grave of his ancestor. He had the purification medicine normally prepared for a grave rubbed directly onto their bodies. Thereafter he gave them cattle from his vast herds, thus weaning them from the need to eat human flesh, and thereby ending cannibalism.

"Moshesh installed his village on *Thaba Bosiu,* a mountain that is not very high, but crowned with near-vertical cliffs, yielding no access to the summit on which lay a plateau with water and good grazing, and where the chief later had a stone house built. Part of this plateau was unaccountably covered with fine white sand, such as one might only find on a beach. *Thaba Bosiu* became an impenetrable fortress that seemed to loom larger at night, and hence became known as the *Mountain of the Night*. Moshesh's formidable reputation as a chief warrior spread throughout the country."

The Qiloane pinnacle, close to Thaba Bosiu

Thaba Bosiu mountain (left) and the Qiloane (right)

The conical grass-woven Basotho hat resembles the shape of the Qiloane pinnacle.

A creative model could also be unique!

Chris relates how her spiritual lineage was intimately linked with the generous, courteous and wise King, Moshesh.

"It is 1833. The history of this region is shaping itself. Three ardent French Protestant missionaries of the *Société des missions évangéliques de Paris*, (the Paris Evangelical Missionary

Society) - Eugène Casalis (21), Thomas Arbousset (23) and Constant Gosselin (32) - set out for southern Africa fired with a passionate determination to share their faith, their knowledge and their crafts.

"In Lesotho, Moshesh not only had to deal with the invading Zulus, but also with the Boers who were moving up north, and he was getting tired of the incessant wars. While the missionaries were making their way from Port Elizabeth up through southern Africa, Moshesh met a Griqua hunter named Adam Krotz, who came from the Christian community of Philippolis, free from invasions. So Moshesh asked him for guns with which to better protect his people. But being a Christian, Krotz replied that he would do better by asking the help of the missionaries who could show him the way of peace between tribes."

Moshesh had never seen Whites and did not know what missionaries were. But he instructed Adam Krotz to find and bring him at least one of these servants of the unknown God, and entrusted him with two hundred cattle to conclude the contract!

The cattle were stolen three times! But when the missionaries arrived in Philippolis where Adam Krotz lived, he was finally able to deliver the message. These courageous men took this as divine guidance, and followed Adam Krotz to *Thaba Bosiu*, where on June 28, 1833 they finally met the King of the Basotho.

Moshesh found them a place in a lovely valley on the slopes of Makhoarane, not far from his stronghold. The missionaries named it Morija, which for them, meant: "God will provide!" and there built a primitive structure, which they called their first *home*.

Moshesh placed them under the protection of some of his young sons and some men. While Gosselin directed practical activities such as building, water supply, farming, the Basotho helpers would look after the cattle and provide meat through hunting.

The missionaries learned the language (which until then existed only in an oral form) and opened several schools. They prepared reading sheets, primers (1837, 1839) and a small book of prayers (1837); a small catechism (1836), and translated the Gospels of Mark and John, followed by some 50 chapters of the Bible, and had them printed in Cape Town (1839). Casalis wrote the first grammar of the Sotho language (1841). The first 28 hymns were printed on the small mission press at Beersheba in 1843.

Moshesh followed the development of these activities with great interest. He was particularly appreciative of their role as advisers in his dealings with the Boers and with the British Administrators of the time.

And it was in Morija that the Paris Evangelical Missionary Society established its Headquarters. About 40 years later, this village became the centre of various institutions such as a Printing works and Bookshop, a Teacher Training College, a Bible School for evangelists, and a Theological Seminary.

SUTOLAND. — Morija.   Phot. Dr. G. Hertig

Morija, the oldest village in Lesotho

Thus Morija became known as *Selibeng sa Thuto*, The Fountain of Learning.

After various other missions, Chris's father became Head of the Theological Seminary of Morija in 1927 at the age of fifty-nine, and held the post until his retirement in 1934. So he and his family lived in the house beside the institution. Chris retained loving memories of it to the end of her days.

"There were the wonderful trees planted by

the first missionaries: a marvelous fig tree with white figs, cherry trees, apricot trees, and vines that yielded enormous grapes. There were also apple, quince and peach trees, nectarines, a medlar, a big mulberry tree, a huge pear tree in front of the house, and several pomegranate and almond trees. We were particularly fond of the beautiful pines at the back of the garden, the kernels of which we ate, and the decorative pepper plant with its fine leaves and bright little red grains.

"There were cows and three horses in the adjoining terrain. All our outings had to be on horseback. (It took my sister five hours to reach home on horseback.) There were no shops in Morija, apart from the stores that sold the colored blankets worn by Basotho men and women over their clothing regardless of the season, and held together with a big safety pin. The horses would wait patiently outside the store, while their owners sold the wool from their sheep and the product of their fields, in exchange for flour and other necessities.

"Missionaries lived on a very small salary, almost without money. They had to be self-sufficient and had to have reserves, especially as they had to be ready at all times to cater for unexpected visitors. We had chickens, two turkeys and pigs. We always had a lot of milk and my mother made butter. She also made jams, preserves, jars of big peaches yellow and firm, sausages and ham. Life was good and we never lacked for anything. As children we were carefree and lived in the Land of Plenty."

But if life was good, there were also some less pleasant surprises: one such was the plague of locusts.

"No sooner had the locusts landed, than everything was devoured. Not a leaf or green shoot was left. What they did leave behind was the lament of the population, devastated fields, lost harvests and guaranteed famine in the near future. The people grew thin. Nevertheless, the Basotho tried to make the best out of this calamity. They collected the thousands of the locusts that had fallen, suffocated and squashed. Once the legs, wings and heads were torn off, the innards emptied and grilled, they did not taste too bad. Ground into a kind of flour, they kept a long time and supplemented ordinary fare."

"I also tried them," Chris continued, "but did not particularly care for the taste!"

After this digression, Chris continued to relate the history of the country of her birth.

"Lesotho never became part of South Africa, but economically it was closely linked. There was little work in Lesotho and agriculture was at the mercy of frequent bouts of drought. The Basotho could not live solely of their meager herds of cattle and sheep, so they had to go and work in South Africa to labor under the earth. For nine months, the free men they had been became slaves of the gold mines, during which they were crammed into the mine *compounds*, that is, dormitories for men. At the end of their contract they would return to their families for their annual three months' holiday. But being forced to expatriate themselves in this way had devastating effects for some."

Chris let her mind meander between her past and the present. At times she described the events in the retirement home with wry humor.

"At Christmas they lined us all up in the dining-room, and one by one, we had to go up to the director to get a kiss."

I spent a week with Chris in Paris a few months before she passed away. She was in a wheelchair then and her hands had become so fragile, that she had to be assisted at mealtimes. But she had not lost her sense of humor.

One day, with a twinkle in her eye, Chris told me, "You know, some people hold very strange conversations. All they say to one is: 'Open your mouth!' and 'Shut your mouth!'"

Chris had a very sharp sense of observation, and if she spoke less, she still noticed what was going on and would suddenly come out with some witty remark. Then our laughter would ring out in the whole dining-room.

On my last day, a very dignified and cultured lady resident with whom I had hitherto had no personal contact, walked over to our table, and smiling at me, said, "Your presence here has cheered up all of us."

By contrast to the drab daily routine, Chris's inner life was rich and profound. Her commitment to selfless service, her daily study of the Living Word by which she lived her life - ("How I would love to learn these sentences off by heart, but my memory is going to pot!") - and her deep concern for the South Africa she so ardently loved, were the themes that were reflected in her dreams.

Chris's second elephant dream occurred the day after the first.

I find myself alone in the back of beyond in the Transkei, one of the zones in South Africa reserved for Blacks. I am feeling utterly distraught; (.....) and the bus has left without me. I don't know where I am, or where I am going, or what direction to take. I join three or four other people and make my way with them. (...).

I find myself in a country scene I know well, walking in the opposite direction. I meet two Black countrywomen. They are barefooted and wear the long flared skirt worn by every African woman in this region. I tell them that I have got lost. They are kind, willing to help, and tell me to accompany them. (...). The color of the earth is ochre; on the left there is a row of tall eucalyptus trees. In front of us, on the right, rises a little hill with very green grass, in contrast to the rare tufts of long grass around us that have been scorched by the cold. We walk in silence.

All of a sudden I see, arriving from the hillock on our right and diagonally crossing the path in front of us towards the left, an extraordinary apparition.

I cannot believe my eyes. It is an enormous elephant, extremely tall, with gaunt flanks. His huge head leans forward, his massive hunched shoulders make one think of a mastodon. His legs are disproportionately long and thin. The top of his head, with his enormous ears and trunk, is a luminous azure blue.

All the rest of his head, from ears to trunk, body and tail, is as if lacquered a brilliant royal blue, with a glint of enamel. One could have thought that to separate the two colors, a line had been drawn with a gigantic ruler the whole length of his body.

The elephant is a veteran, yet he has a very bizarre gait like that of an awkward young elephant. It is (...) as if he walks on the air about thirty centimeters above the ground. Without a glance in our direction, he crosses the path in front of us and disappears in the valley on our left.

I am flabbergasted, but feel no fear.

In the dream itself I become aware that what I see is a fantastic vision, altogether different from the pale green elephants that were definitely of this world!

Dumbfounded, I turn to the woman walking on my right and say to her in French, "Did you see him?"

"Yes," she replies calmly. Then she adds: "He is not real, you know. It is an idea in your head."

Taken aback, I ask, after a moment's silence: "And you, what did you see?"

"An enormous elephant," she replied, "azure and royal blue, who came from the direction of the green hill

on the right, and who crossed the path in front of us diagonally, before descending on the left. He was walking on the air, about thirty centimeters above the ground."

Astonished, I reflect on this reply, becoming aware in my dream how strange it is, that she should have seen the same thing as I, when in fact, she told me it was an idea in my head.

On an impulse, I ask her: "Have you seen him before?"

"No," she replied. "But my grandmother, she has seen him!"

End of the dream.
A Mystery!

Chris interprets her dream:

The elephant has always been for me the symbol of Africa, and therefore, of the African. All these elephants had gaunt flanks, which I took to signify the hunger, the profound misery, of the Blacks around us. It was probably my permanent preoccupation about my country that led to this dream.

The woman and I are intimately connected. It is significant that she is Black. In the South African context, I always tried to identify with Black people. The woman says the elephant is not real. He is tall - which suggests a high ideal. But the vision is fantastic: it symbolizes an ideal, but not a reality. But is closeness and understanding an unrealistic ideal?

The Black woman beside me has never seen this ideal in action before. But her grandmother has: she has seen the fantastic elephant. Her grandmother would have lived in the time before the onset of Nationalism in 1948, before the racial discrimination laws came into force, when schools and universities were still mixed, and before relationships and marriage between persons of different color had been forbidden by law. At that time Coloreds and Blacks were still represented in the government, and there still existed some harmonious relationships between Whites and Blacks.

These dreams resulted from my ardent desire for a multiracial society in South Africa, in which people would live in harmony and mutual understanding; in contrast to the fear and retribution about to descend. If these dreams have taught me nothing new about myself, they illustrate the marvelous ingenuity with which the dream transforms an idea into an image, and interpreting one's dreams can become a fascinating pastime available to all.

As her friend, I could not help wondering if there could not be a greater meaning to the dream of the big blue elephant. Where did the symbol come from? Did it exist in the Basotho culture? But no, I found none. For Chris, the colors of the green and blue elephant were mainly symbolic of unresolved racial issues.

But the big blue elephant was more mysterious. Was there a greater dimension to this dream? What might a further search reveal?

Chris had already nursed one older sister till she passed on; but caring for this doubly infirm old lady was far more demanding. She lived on the meager budget provided by her brother-in-law, and stretched it by strict economies such as hand-washing her sister's clothes daily, even with her increasingly painful arthritic hands. It was only when Chris had become too weak to lift her sister, and only then, that the retirement home finally provided extra nursing aid.

I admired Chris enormously. She did not yield to fatigue or pain, nor let the situation put an end to her intellectual pursuits. She would set her alarm for midnight, go to sleep at ten p.m., sleep for two hours, and wake to read great French literature till two in the morning. Then, next morning without fail, she would face her sister's daily nursing routine all over again. In time her hands became too painful to hold large books. Then she simply found a way to prop them up and continued her studies nonetheless.

We were both ageing.

I visited Chris as often as I could, but I lived in Geneva and she in Paris.

"I want to live victoriously," she repeated as her life got tougher. Only rarely did she mention that it was hard.

Chris was much loved during her lifetime. She had made friends wherever she went, and even one belated *best* friend in the home.

"I didn't know one could make such a good friend so late in life."

Letters from past students arrived from all

over the world. But she lived long on after her sister's death, and likewise outlived most of her friends. I seemed to be the last one who knew her business. A year before she died, Chris entrusted me to look after her documents, and that is how I discovered that her South African identity card needed to be renewed.

So I travelled to Paris once more, and early one morning we set out by taxi to go to the South African Embassy on the Quai d'Orsay. Chris loved the ride through Paris.

When we arrived, we could not get Chris and her wheelchair through the front door. But two kind men rushed out of the embassy and carried her up the steps through the back entrance and into the lift. The atmosphere was informal. We were asked to wait in the comfortable waiting room, and a lady came to take Chris's fingerprints. She was gentle and kind, but the hands that had served so long and so well were so deformed that Chris's inked fingers could not all touch the paper at the same time.

When the formalities had been completed, the young African consul and his assistant came to sit and to chat with us informally. Chris spoke to him in a gentle, loving way, and in the African tradition towards the elderly, he was deeply respectful. Though he came from the north, he also spoke Sesotho.

In no time at all they were smiling and exchanging news, as among old friends.

Suddenly Chris burst into song. The gentle, soft-spoken consul and his assistant joined her in the familiar and cherished words and their hearts united as they sang.

Lesotho National Anthem

Lesotho fatse la bontat'a rona,
Har'a mafatse le letle ke lona.
Ke moo re hlahileng,
Ke moo re holileng,
Rea la rata.
Molimo ak'u boloke Lesotho,
U felise lintoa le matsoenyeho.
Oho fatse lena,
La bontat'a rona,
Le be le khotso.

Lesotho, land of our Fathers,
You are the most beautiful country of all.
You give us birth,
In you we are reared
And you are dear to us.
Lord, we ask You to protect Lesotho.
Keep us free from conflict and tribulation.
Oh, land of mine,
Land of our Fathers,
May you have peace.

This anthem, it seems to me, holds the key to Chris's life: her Christian upbringing; her youth rooted in a multi-racial milieu in which she identified with and had an ardent love for the Africans; her fervent belief that all men are equal, and her passionate activism.

After her death, I got in touch with Chris's remaining relatives. Her nephew, Roger Nixon, asked me to write something about her life. But it was to take several years to fill in the gaps and gain a deeper understanding of the historical background, and the culture in which Chris's life had been anchored.

Relentless in the demands she had made on herself, Chris had kept faith through innumerable difficulties, and found solace in prayer. She had served unselfishly and with love. But it had been hard.

She had soldiered her way through the long grey tunnel of the retirement home, nursing her sister till she passed away. By then her back was in constant pain, and in time her legs became too weak to serve her. Chris bore her suffering with courage and serenity. But she never lost the essential gaiety that always emerged whenever I visited her in the home.

Chris lived on for many years thereafter and was both appreciated and loved. She continued to study and pay keen attention to news about the evolution of South Africa and the Africans she identified with, loved and had helped as much as she had been able.

My thoughts were often drawn back to the enormous blue elephant. How was it connected to the kind of life she had lived? Did he send an even deeper message?

I meant to track it down. I enquired here and sought there, but could find no other reference to a big, blue elephant until the Hindu god Ganesha, Remover of Obstacles and Patron of the arts and sciences, came to mind. He is a deity with an elephant head, represented as blue or on a blue background.

Does the unconscious dip into one Source for all cultures? Did the dream bypass religious beliefs, and tune into something mysterious, mystical and divine?

A long search left me with the two recurring basic symbols: the *elephant* and the color *blue*.

The elephant represents something very big. Blue represents truth, wisdom, devotion, tranquility, loyalty, heaven and eternity; it is the color of the Divine. In her last dream, these themes merged. Had not her very life been like the enormous blue elephant?

Then Chris shared her third dream-vision with the residents. It had stayed with her so clearly, that she had not felt the need to write it down.

It is the most beautiful dream I have ever had, and I remember it as if it was yesterday, although it is years since I had it, and I never wrote it down. It is a scenario;

there is no action.

I found myself in a small and quite ordinary room with only three walls. They were drab and grey: there were no objects of any kind or furniture. I could divine the scene beyond the fourth wall, but I could not actually see it.

Up on the wall on my left there hung a kind of picture in a very large pewter frame, in the centre of which, as if embedded in the neutral background, there rose a circle about five centimeters high. It was not a painting, not a collage, not metal, enamel or a gem. It was Light of a wondrous blue, more vivid than azure, a living Light that pulsated radiance.

The dream was about the effect this Light had on me. I had not the slightest doubt that it represented Paradise, Life Eternal. I could not believe how happy I was; FREE, free of any burden, weightless; sustained in my element as a fish in water, as a bird in flight. I had experienced a sort of revelation in the dream. It illumined all the days that followed.

Chris's journey through the long, grey tunnel had come to an end. She had lived like a warrior and had completed the task that had brought her to Paris. Her nephew, Roger Nixon, wrote: "The strength of purpose which the missionaries derived from their faith was replicated in her."

Just two months before her ninetieth birthday, Chris suddenly took ill and had to be taken into hospital. The pastor was sent for, and went to be with her. "Mrs. Nixon recognized me when I arrived and welcomed my presence," he told me later. "She was conscious almost right up to the end."

On October 30, 2005, Hélène Nixon-Christeller passed away. Breaking the chains of limitation, she had found freedom in a higher perspective. And yet, profoundly humble, she would never have accepted any suggestion that her life had been unusual. *"C'est la vie!"*

But her soul knew! It had taken flight into higher realms and had sent its message of comfort in the two symbols close to her heart: the unforgettable expanse of blue above her African home, and Africa's largest mammal. She had been visited by the Big Blue Elephant, and had bathed in the Light of Blue. For me, her life was, and remains, a tremendous inspiration.

My gratitude goes to all those who helped me in my efforts to do honor to Chris's life: her nephew in Belfast, her niece in Geneva and her friends. I was also privileged to meet a couple of missionary colleagues who had, for thirty-five years, lived and worked in Morija, and who now live in Switzerland. Though they do not wish to be named, I must express my gratitude, for they not only supplied me with much additional information about the life and work of the missionaries, but patiently read and verified my numerous versions, as I tried to find the words that would do justice to Chris's life.

QUEEN OF COMPASSION

"Love is an *illusion*," my wise old Uncle told me. I set out to disprove this unpalatable statement. The resulting quest was to take me halfway round the world.

The East! My last Sunday in Singapore. The young man who is my guide speaks to me earnestly. He has only one desire - to take me to a certain temple he knows. He has been saving this visit for the end. I am not enthusiastic and he is not able to make me so.

We leave the hotel and cross the main road; walking is easy and comfortable here. Streets are clean, and the strict laws against pollution have had their effect. A big blue Dragon's head towers above a building; but we pass it by.

"The small temple is down a back street," he says, "and tourists don't go there."

He leads me down a narrow road and we arrive at a low, plain building. The temple is a bare, rectangular room; the door is half open. Plain wooden benches are stacked in a corner and paint-stained planks lie scattered around. A man is up a ladder; an open pot of paint stands on the floor. The only thing missing is an Out of Order sign.

A smiling woman arrives in a grey robe. There is a hint of grey stubble on the shorn head. She ushers us in.

"You must take your shoes off first," my guide tells me. I don't like having to walk barefoot in this. Soon stuff sticks to the soles of my feet.

"She is a Buddhist nun," he says, "and the voice for Kuan Yin."

(Many of Singapore's temples used to have a resident spiritual medium).

I have never heard of Kuan Yin. I cannot even spell the name.

As the temple is being redecorated, the medium cannot work today. My guide informs me that she wears rich robes and full headgear for the formal Sunday service; it is only then that she functions as Kuan Yin's spokesperson and transmits her messages. He did not tell me, then, that he was himself a trance medium in training, and that the goddess had spoken to him. My guide and the nun converse rapidly; it really is Chinese. From time to time the young man turns to me briefly, and says something in English.

The Buddhist nun goes to the back of the Temple, and returns with sweets and tea.

"She says she does not want you to have come here today for nothing," he tells me, looking very pleased.

The hot tea does me a lot of good and I drink it gratefully, while they talk animatedly in Chinese, with frequent pokes in my direction.

"She says she will pray for you," my interpreter tells me. I hadn't asked to be prayed for! Besides, what would be use of praying for *me*?

The Buddhist nun disappears into the back room, and returns holding an object I cannot identify. The two of them converse in some excitement. No one bothers to translate anything for me. The nun goes to stand behind my chair. Suddenly something hard and wet lands on the back of my neck.

"She has stamped you!" he tells me.

Drops begin to trickle down my back. I raise my hand to wipe my neck.

"Don't touch it! You must leave it to dry."

I do not realize that my neck now bears a large round reddish stamp and that I will return to the hotel looking like a prize cheese.

Later I discover an article on the web: "Pilgrimage in Contemporary China," wherein Chün-Fang Yü relates that "on pilgrimages to sacred sites red seals were stamped on the bags and belts indicating the monasteries the people had visited. When they die, they would be (...) cremated together with the incense bags and belts. These would serve as "travel passes" and would assure them a safe journey to Paradise."

I see!

The temperature is 30° centigrade. I feel hot, bothered and very uncomfortable. There is still stuff sticking to the soles of my feet. The Buddhist nun smiles at me and fetches more tea, thick with sugar. For this I really am grateful. She goes to the back of the Temple once more and returns with a gift: it is a small ferryboat.

"It's for the great crossing," my guide tells me.

I don't feel like a crossing - great or small: all I want now is to get back to my hotel.

The Buddhist nun seeks my eyes and smiles at me once more; then she gives me a dark poster portraying a white deity.

I roll the poster up and thank the nun. My restlessness increases: I want to leave.

But my guide and the nun go on talking; it is still about me. They are looking very pleased. I can't for the life of me see what there is to be so pleased about.

I get up to go. Just before we leave the nun brings me the gift of a second boat. That makes two fragile ferryboats to pack: my safe journey to the farthest shore is now assured.

Time to return to Europe: time to pack. Finally everything fits into my fuchsia travelling bag, except this poster. I look at it again; it is glossy and cheap! Might as well leave it behind; it's only a poster. Or give it to the porter! Perhaps I'll try just one more time: I roll up a towel, roll the poster around that, then roll my skirt around that, and finally squeeze the bundle into my bag.

The poster travels well. By the time I unpack it in Geneva it has been *antiqued*. Fine cracks run across the thick, glossy paper, making it look like parchment. I look at it more closely. A majestic bejeweled Chinese deity, clad in a flowing white robe, stands barefoot on the back of a long dragon with shiny emerald scales, a belly edged in bronze, and a copper mane. He has ivory antler horns, large onyx eyes, a flaring crimson tongue, sharp white teeth, two long golden whiskers that spread out like feelers from his wide open snout, a wispy green beard, and four ferocious claws. (In China only the Emperor was allowed to possess a dragon with *five* claws). Kuan Yin wears a necklace; high above her head, her black hair is crested by a tiara. In her left hand she holds a precious golden vase from which flows some nectar. Her right hand, palm facing outwards, is raised in a sacred gesture (*mudra*).

I frame the poster behind anti-reflection glass, hang it in our living room opposite the front door, and begin to look up at the graceful goddess riding her dragon through the clouds in a blaze of light.

"But who is she?" I had asked my young guide, back there in Singapore.

Photo ©Emmanuel Power

Kuan Yin - Queen of Compassion

"Kuan Yin is a Celestial Bodhisattva whose job it is to help the Buddha. In Sanskrit her name means, The One who Hears the Sounds (Cries) of the World and Comes."

"But what exactly *is* a Bodhisattva?"

"A being who has overcome the world by the practice of strict disciplines (spiritual perfections) and who no longer needs to incarnate. But because of infinite compassion for suffering humanity, a Bodhisattva forgoes the bliss of Union with the Divine, and chooses to stay close to the earth in her transcendent state, to help all beings unconditionally. In this way Kuan Yin has become Captain of the "Bark of Salvation" who ferries humans safely across the sea of suffering. She will go to a thousand places, respond to a thousand prayers and alleviate a thousand fears.

But in Mahayana Buddhism there are two kinds of Bodhisattvas: the second kind is that of the lay follower who aspires to enlightenment and dedicates (him-) herself to the service of mankind by endeavoring to be loving and compassionate to all sentient beings alike."

Here it is again - this thing about the bliss of Union with the Divine: I've heard it before!

My life has now claimed five decades. Young loves have come and gone; older love too. Heart has opened and shut. But I still believe: love is *not* an illusion! I assemble the fragments of memory and experience; suddenly, I'm twenty!

"There is an excellent esoteric library in London," my Uncle tells me. "As you are looking for Truth, you might find some interesting books there. Go to the Baker Street Underground next to Madame Tussaud's Waxworks, cross the street and walk down Gloucester Place towards Marble Arch."

In the musty library I borrow a novel about the love affair of a human and an immortal. In the hall below some public lectures are about to begin. Next week there's one that's an absolute must. It's on Love!

There are ten chairs across, five on each side of the aisle, and eight rows down in the small lecture hall. My seat is in the third row on the right, next to a friend – far too near the front.

The speaker, a widow, is around seventy, has white hair down to her shoulders and a powerful build. She has just come back from her second pilgrimage to India where she spent six months with her guru. Her plain black dress is lit by the gaudy broach that glitters below her neck and captures one's gaze as she begins to speak, till only her voice remains. Vigorously she embarks on the subject of love.

I am still hoping to find someone who will confirm that love is *not* an illusion; maybe this Russian woman will. I hope she will prove the others wrong.

Love is - she quotes the Scriptures...
Love is - she quotes Eastern texts...

Yes, yes, yes! Go on! Go on!

Love is the most wonderful thing on earth!

I have come to the right place!

Her voice warms till it begins to glow.

Love is ... she continues and quotes the ultimate heights ever known to humankind.

Great! Great! Great! So, love is *not* an illusion!

I sit back and relax. At last, someone has said exactly what I wanted to hear!

Now the speaker is into the heart of her subject. Her body sways with the surge of it. She has experienced the love she describes, and it surges forth for all to see!

"And then - after all the most wondrous experiences - love takes one further, beyond anything ever imagined. And you fly high in the sky - wizz Love!"

I can just see it: Up and Away!

A wave surges through my body, rises to a crest; foam-spray glistens in the sun. My stifled ribs begin to ache. I daren't look at my friend; we can hardly hold our laughter.

The lecture continues in crescendo. The fine silver hair is drawn back severely, and the cheap broach glitters at her neck.

"And I tell you, my friends, LOVE IS ALL."

Here we are at last! So love is *not* an illusion after all.

Suddenly there is a lull.

The speaker's gaze sweeps across the room and then stops to scrutinize each of us in turn. There is a long, deep silence.

"But," the passionate voice rises, "there is *no such thing* as love!"

She begins to speak about her experience at the feet of her guru. "There is no greater love than the Union of the Soul with the Beloved."

Can't one even find love without having to go through all that with a guru?

"The greatest love affair on this earth," she concludes, "is the love of the Soul for the Divine."

Back in our flat in Geneva, possibly I emerge from my reverie – as determined as before: Love *cannot* be an illusion!

Kuan Yin still rides the dragon with the shiny emerald scales (said to be 117 in number; 36 yin and 81 yang!), and I've grown accustomed to the poster on the wall. It is the first thing I see when I walk through the front door and I've learned to live with her. But everything has changed; now she seems breathtakingly beautiful.

One particularly hard day I wonder: Can it be true as John Bloefeld suggests in *Bodhisattva of Compassion*, that all one needs to do is to call out Kuan Yin's name, and she'll be here? Is it true that: "Rocks, willows, lotus pools or running water are often indications of her presence. In the chime of bronze or jade, the sigh of wind in the pines, the prattle and tinkle of streams, her voice is heard."

"Kuan Yin," I call out one day, "Kuan Yin."

Is she real? Or is she Myth? Can an archetypal symbol be taken from one culture and transposed to another?

"Kuan Yin, can you hear me?"

She does not move; she does not speak. But I begin to feel dreamy, happy, consoled. A fragrant mist wafts in. The floor carpets itself in white; the delicate fragrance of gardenia fills the room. I fill with pleasure; welcome its caress. I look around; but I am alone. No one else is home. I look up at Kuan Yin, and my heart beats one with her.

Forgotten words, once whispered to me, now slip back into my mind.

Compassion is the elder sister of love.

A year later I find myself in Boston for two weeks on a course: I'm walking along the street, with nothing particular in mind. My eye catches the figure of a white Madonna in the window of a small art and curio shop. I go in to ask.

"Oh, that's Kuan Yin. We have a book about her. Would you like to browse through it?" An oriental gentleman leads me to a table and armchair behind a curtain at the back of the shop, hands me a book, and leaves me to read. A little later he comes back with a cup of green tea. I thank him.

This is fascinating! There is even such a thing as a Kuan Yin initiation into cosmic sound. As I walk down the street, spring is in my step. So, Kuan Yin is in Boston, too!

I get the feel of a little shrine, somewhere, not far from here. I walk down unfamiliar streets, following the inner trail. After a while I see an orange-robed monk disappearing around the corner. The next day I return to the same area, and walk around. Presently two orange-robed monks appear, but they, too, seem to vanish. I go to the area Supermarket and ask the tall Security guard.

"Oh yes, I've see them, too," he says. "They seem to come from somewhere behind there." He points in the direction of a large apartment block, and I make my way towards them. I recall the fragrance of gardenias. I want to find the Buddhist Madonna; I want to find her here. I loiter around, wondering what to do next. Then I see an old man, and ask him if he knows of a Kuan Yin temple.

"In that building there," he says, indicating a door a few paces away. I find it on the third floor. A well-rounded monk with kind face and stubble of grey hair opens the door.

"Kuan Yin?"

His eyes nearly pop out of his head.

"Quan Âm."

"Me, meditation," I say, joining my hands and bowing.

The Venerable ushers me in.

"Japanese?"

"Vietnam."

The front room serves as temple and meditation room. A tall, white statue of Kuan Yin stands on a cloth-covered table. A trickle of incense rises and wafts through the room.

"Hallo," I say to her, "So it's you!"

Discretely the Buddhist Master leaves the room. I sit down on the floor in front of Kuan Yin and wait. I make no promises; do not bargain. Yet before I call I am answered.

A stack of little cards lies beside the incense. Each is a miniature replica of the poster given to me in the small Kuan Yin temple in Singapore.

When I'm ready to leave the Venerable gives me one of the little cards and says, "You come tomorrow afternoon, five o'clock. Speak English. Good!"

The following day there were seven pairs of Buddhist sandals by the door. The grey-robed lay members had just completed the closing ritual of a strenuous retreat, and were taking light refreshments in the kitchen, which they immediately offered to share with me. One of them could speak English and their Spiritual Director asked her to translate.

We all sat on the floor. Then the Venerable's deep, guttural voice burst out:

"How did you find us? We only moved here a few months ago. No European has ever set foot in here before!"

I told the story at great length. How I had seen a statue of Kuan Yin in the art and curio shop, just up the road; how I had followed the trail. How, just one year before that, my guide had taken me to her temple in Singapore; what an awful mood I had been in; how my neck had been stamped; how I brought the poster to Geneva. And how, a year later, Kuan Yin's fragrance had filled my home.

From time to time the Venerable interjected comments of his own. These were not translated for me, but made everyone smile - at each other - and at me.

It had got late. People were tired after the strenuous disciplines of the last days, and needed to get home. As I ended my story the Venerable held me in his forceful gaze, then he addressed me thus: "All this can only mean one thing: you, too, must become a Bodhisattva."

He must have meant the second kind, but still... *thirty-seven* practices and *five* merits!

One by one the members of the group left. I thanked the Venerable and slipped out.

WHEN THE LARGE WHITE FLAKES FELL

B ack through my life...

I was a child once. My parents dreamt of giving me the best education, and black-and-white nuns willingly delivered it. Lips were for murmuring matins; mouths were best kept shut.

And one should never, never indulge in daydreams. The regime was that of guilt and shame.

Apart from the priest, the only male around was the Italian gardener with a wooden leg, who played the accordion on a Friday night - so beautifully, that we all fell in love with him!

Our slender necks hung in halters; the nuns shaped our souls.

But it was the lay Drama teacher who, drawing on what was seen as wisdom in 1912, bequeathed us the female model for life.

We had to repeat and repeat *The Lay of the Health Visitor* until every word had sunk into our heads, designed to remain there for ever.

Indeed, the rhymes sank into the depths of my soul!

The Lay of the Health Visitor

Anna Maria Sophia Jones
Was just a bundle of skin and bones -
The sort of woman you often meet
With knobbledy fingers and large, flat feet -
Her hair was tied behind in a bunch,
And she had dinner when you have lunch.
The Government Lady came to the door -
With printed leaflets - dozens and more.
She spoke to Maria firmly and long -
And all that Maria did was wrong.

She oughtn't to peel potatoes and boil them;
To peel potatoes was only to spoil them;
She oughtn't to waste the pods of the pea;
She oughtn't to stew and stew her tea;
She oughtn't to feed her baby on bread
Before it had ever a tooth in its head.

(Anna Sophia, mother of five,
Three were dead, but two were alive,
Always had given her baby bread
Before it had ever a tooth in its head.)

She oughtn't to spend her money on drink,
She oughtn't to stuff up the drain of her sink;
She oughtn't to shut out air and light;
She oughtn't to close her window at night.

(Anna Maria Sophia Jones
Always fastened her window – click

216

Air in a bedroom made her sick;
She oughtn't to buy herself ready - made clothes
She oughtn't, she oughtn't – Oh goodness knows.)
Before the Government Lady had ended
Anna Sophia was highly offended.

Anna Maria Sophia Jones
Was just a bundle of skin and bones -
The sort of woman you often meet
With knobbledy fingers and large, flat feet -
Her hair was dragged behind in a bunch,
And she had dinner when you have lunch.
But Anna Maria had spirit within her -
The spirit that makes a saint of a sinner.
When she saw what was right she went and did it
And then, if need was, afterward hid it.

Anna Maria Sophia Jones
Asked, in dull and colorless tones
The Government Lady to walk inside,
Opened the door of the passage wide,
Took a chopper and hit her hard,
And buried the body in the yard.

That is virtually all I can remember of the
education in that school.

We slept in anonymous beds in our
anonymous dormitories, ironing the while our
pleated navy-blue serge uniforms under our
mattresses. In the far end of the grounds, the
unfathomable swimming pool was slimy green.

That accounts for six years.

217

The second convent school was somewhat better than the first; only one nun was sadistic. Draped in dull terra cotta uniforms, there was little to distinguish the girls from the dreary red dust of the arid Karoo. Pool there was none.

Once free of boarding school - forever – I took to spinning dreams, while life shunted me this way and that. I dreamt of living in a big house in the country with my family and our animals and to step out in the morning, barefoot, onto real grass. But that dream did not grow up as fast as the rest of us. Nor had it landed by the time of adolescent revolt. Clashingly, time passed. Then the boys went out into the world, leaving behind a dog and a cat. And, tasks accomplished, we, the big ones, parted and went on our separate ways, forever friends. The dog died, and the cat and I had still not managed to live in a house with a garden.

That accounts for the next forty years.

Then, when I least expected it, my dream sailed in. Friends offered me their country house for six months: a large, square, former school house. It stood in isolated rapture up a mountain, body in mist and head in the sun, in proud testimony of days gone by. Overnight I became the solitary mistress of twelve beds, unoccupied, bar one. I turned the living-room into a concert hall, and watched the sun rise over the Mont-Blanc. But I had forgotten to specify that my house in the country was to come with a man in it, and at least one maid!

I needed Bobbie, then, our sleek black cat. I needed her to live with me. She came from that oasis of love that ripens human hearts and had been with us for ten years. *Baba* we had called her - for short.

It only took Bobbie twenty-four hours to settle in. She took to the house and the garden as if she had waited for this all her life. She did not care about cobwebs on her whiskers, the freaky wiring or buzzing flies. But she was captivated by the rustling mice, and these kept her busy for hours.

Elegantly she would walk out the front door as soon as I opened it for her, stop to examine the possibilities, and when done exploring, jump back in through the kitchen window. Every morning she would venture a little further, running across the garden to the neighboring fields to play and tumble. She chased butterflies, stalked a myriad flies or flutters and chewed all kinds of grasses. Sometimes she would just park in the front garden and sit stock-still, looking out over the valley below. But whatever she got up to, however far she ventured, Bobbie never stayed out for very long.

Daily she grew more beautiful as she ran lithely across the fields and tasted wild space. In the early morning she would place a paw gently on my cheek and wait for me to move. In the evenings, in front of the fire, she'd leap into my arms and we'd both purr to our hearts' content. For Bobbie this was paradise.

"Oh, I see!" said a friend on hearing this tale. "You've landed in your cat's dream!"

The glowing autumn turned into the cold of winter. The paraffin heater belched black smoke and gave up. Bobbie rushed out one day into a downpour, and shot back in again with loud complaint. A few days later tentative little paw marks edged the first light flakes of snow.

Then one Sunday in January at four o'clock, *Baba* asked to go out. I picked her up tenderly, removed a grain of sand from the corner of her eyes and said, "There, you're all beautiful now for your adventure." Then I shut the front door quickly as the icy cold seeped in, and pulled the thick curtain across.

Two hours later she had not returned. Suffocating dense fog blinded space. I tried to look for her, but could not see my own feet. I called and called her - again and yet again - at six, at seven, at nine, at midnight. But all to no avail. Nor had she come back by next morning when I had to leave.

Word was sent round that the local farmers had been sprinkling the grass around their homes with rat poison.

The fog had cleared when I got back at four that afternoon. I found Bobbie stiff in the garden – lying head down on the steps that led past the shed. It must have been from there that she had sent out her last faint call in the impenetrable fog of the night before.

I called my husband and my younger son to join me. We stood together as with sharp, jagged strokes my son drove his pickaxe into the earth and laid her in that crumbling crypt under a young birch tree. My older son also needed to be told. He lived too far to come, but he, too, had been attached to Bobbie.

Then one day a terrible snowstorm unfurled. Large crystalline flakes enlaced the young birch tree, veiled the lonely contours of the school house and covered the land.

Time froze and locked me, like an ice maiden, into the white solitude of my mountain retreat. The view of the Mont-Blanc from my bedroom window was breathtaking, but it had no power to warm my heart.

I had lived my dream and had gathered in the fruits of solitude. I will never again need to hanker after a big house in the country.

When the large white flakes fell, our *Baba* lay under the earth, and my heart kept aching.

When the green of spring returned at last, I moved back to the city.

But part of my heart remained under the earth, beside my *Baba*.

CAMINO ENCOUNTERS

Photo ©Emmanuel Power

The emblem for the Way of Saint James

At the end of August a few years ago I set out on the Camino de Santiago (the Way of St. James) from the traditional starting point, *Saint-Jean-de-Pied-de-Port* (literally, Saint John at the foot of the mountain pass) to cross the Pyrenees. I carried six people's intentions, including my own: six rolled-up scraps of paper in my money-belt. Come what may, I was going to deposit these in the Cathedral at Santiago de Compostela. And *what may* did come!

Across northern Spain I found that the walking life is simple, basic. It is surprising how little one needs. Everything non-essential has to go.

Put one foot in front of the other; find the arrow; drink a lot, eat a little; reach a Refugio; get a bed; shower, wash clothes; eat; plug ears, sleep. Rummage-'n-pack and - begin again.

There was much for me to learn: how to eat; how to cope with queues; how to deal with wild dogs; how to have a daughter; how to expect the unexpected; how to find answers. And I had to learn fast.

As time went on, the range of my education increased. At one pilgrims' hostel I met a slender German girl from Berlin.

"Yours is the most beautiful name I have ever heard," she said to me. "I will give it to my daughter."

"Oh! I did not realize you are pregnant."

"I am not."

"Well, how do you know you will have a daughter?"

"I just know," she said. "I have the father for her already."

"I did not realize you are married!"

"I am not," she said, "but my boyfriend does not want children."

"He does not?"

"No," she said. "But now I have met a man who does."

"You want to marry him?"

"No," she said. "He has a girlfriend already. But *she* does not want any children!"

"And how are you going to do that while walking all day?"

She looked at me with a little crooked smile.

"One finds everything one needs on the Camino."

Put one foot in front of the other; find the arrow; drink a lot, eat a little; reach a Refugio; get a bed; shower, wash clothes; eat; plug ears, sleep. Rummage-'n-pack and - begin again.

Many pilgrims find what they are looking for. Then they return to give something back. One American found the love of his life and now has a Spanish wife. The couple returns each year to serve for two weeks as *Hospitaleros* in a pilgrim's refuge on the Way. They welcomed me with great friendliness and it was a relief to hear English spoken once more.

Another such person was Carla, a radiant young Brazilian woman. I met her in a small private *Refugio* after walking the first 100 kilometres, when I was dead beat. She took one look at me and said, "I will cook for you tonight," and this felt like Heaven. Carla was passionate about the Camino, and shared her vital experience. "I used to go into Churches looking for Jesus," she told me. "Where are You?" I would ask in one church after the other. I have come from Brazil three times to walk the Camino. But *this* time I found Him. "It is *You*!" I said when I saw *Him*. And He changed my life."

Most magical of all were the unexpected helpers who seemed to pop up out of nowhere. These love the Camino, and are determined to show it. Suddenly, after a hard long climb, one finds a little old lady sitting in front of a ramshackle hut in the street, with a basket of fresh figs - one for each passing pilgrim - or a man at the end of a long field, giving away biscuits and good cheer.

What touched me most, however, was gradually becoming aware of the chain of prayer that sweeps across the Camino path. One can walk for long stretches through farmland, woods and vineyards, without meeting anyone. Then suddenly one will see from the distance, often on top of a hill, a chapel or church spire, such as at Villamayor of Monjardin, and one heads for that. In such places the energy of the Camino is particularly vibrant. There will be a fountain nearby with a bench, and if the chapel is open, it is sure to be cooler inside. Whatever the state of the village, the chapel will be beautifully kept. And in it one will find three or four older women, and perhaps a man or two, praying half aloud, or whispering to their tender- faced Lady and touching Her feet. From hamlet to village, from town to town, I found bouquets of lilies at the Madonna's feet, and always the older women, holding the tradition.

Put one foot in front of the other; find the arrow; drink a lot, eat a little; reach a Refugio; get a bed; shower, wash clothes; eat; plug ears, sleep. Rummage-'n- pack and - begin again.

Before this pilgrimage I thought there was not much hope for the world. But by the end, I knew: as long as there is this chain of prayer across the land, there is hope - much hope.

When at last I got to the Cathedral at Santiago de Compostela, I finally discovered where to put the little scraps of paper bearing intentions. In a side chapel in which stood a statue of Our Lady at one end, is a kneeling, life-sized figure of Jesus, his arms outstretched, his eyes raised towards an angel holding a chalice. An oval basket lies at His knees.

I extracted the six tatty bits of paper I had guarded so long and lit some candles. But the basket did not entice me. I wanted to place them closer, somehow. Looking up, I saw that other people had had the same idea: little scraps of human entreaty lay on His shoulders and along His arms. I placed mine in the palm of His Hands and sat down. It was done.

When I am asked why I undertook this pilgrimage, I find it is virtually impossible to say. The call came, and I went. A Benedictine nun in charge of the Leon *Refugio* was interviewed on local television. "People go on the Camino for four reasons: religious, spiritual, cultural, or simply for adventure. We never worry about their reasons. What is absolutely certain, however, is that the pilgrimage changes them."

On the Way, I also met a young Spaniard who addressed me in English. "Yesterday I had a ticket to the Greek islands. Today I go on the Camino. I have problems with my girlfriend. I will walk for ten days. It will clear my head."

Photo ©Emmanuel Power
The Way of St. James through Switzerland

The Camino has its own way of reaching out and provides its own signals, though one may not always notice them in time.

A few days ago here in Geneva, I was stopped by an elderly pilgrim, not far from my home in the city centre. He was walking to Spain and asked me to show him the Way.

I have lived in this area for ten years, but was not able to do so.

Photo ©Emmanuel Power
The Way of St. James through Geneva

Two days later I noticed it for the first time: the blue and yellow scallop shell, emblem of St. James, high up on a building in a street that crosses mine!

And since then I see them regularly, the pilgrims passing through, with their tired backpacks and scallop shells, some walking light-heartedly, buoyantly even, some at a grim pace: elderly men or a robust young one with a wild bushy beard, or sometimes solitary, wiry women.

And, as they hesitate at the corner and pour over a map, we exchange a smile, and I point the way.

Buen Camino!

CREDITS

Earlier versions of seven of these true stories were published on Editors' Choice, Travelers' Tales website www.travelerstales.com and in 2004 and 2006 in Travelers' Tales books.

Highly Unusual, April 09, 2009

Greek Hospitality, April 24, 2008

Camino Encounters, December 21, 2007

Someone Who Cared, September 04, 2007

The Last Good Woman, October 10, 2006

One Man's Swiss Journey, May 26, 2006

The Ring in The Best Travel Writing 2006

Queen of Compassion in A Woman's Asia, 2004

The Ring, December 22, 2003

About the Author

Sophia Tellen is a student of Life, in the search for underlying truth. She explores the experiences of her life as she moves in and out of countries and cultures, experiences change and meets the challenge of jobs high and low, professional and laic, while becoming a wife, mother, and finally writer. She now gives back and shares the insights and blessings that have accompanied her on her journey.

Other books by Sophia Tellen:

Walking Into Moments

A Blessing From Aymone

Inscribed Upon the Heavens